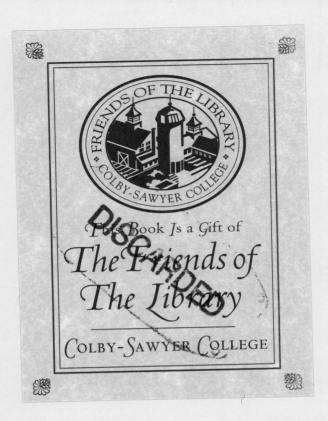

READING
THE JAPANESE
MIND

READING
THE JAPANESE
MIND

The Realities behind
Their Thoughts and Actions

Robert M. March

KODANSHA INTERNATIONAL
Tokyo • New York • London

*Portions of this book have been excerpted for magazine
publication or used as a college text.*

*Distributed in the United States by Kodansha America, Inc.,
114 Fifth Avenue, New York, New York 10011, and in
the United Kingdom
and continental Europe by Kodansha Europe Ltd.,
95 Aldwych, London
WC2B 4JF.*

*Published by Kodansha International Ltd., 17-14 Otowa 1-chome,
Bunkyo-ku, Tokyo 112, and Kodansha America, Inc.*

Library of Congress Cataloguing-in-Publication data pending.

ISBN 4-7700-2044-9

CONTENTS

Introduction   9

1 SOCIAL MAN, *TATEMAE* MAN   19

2 YES MAY MEAN NO:
How the Japanese Communicate   32

3 READING THE JAPANESE MIND:
Ways of Thinking Beyond Logic   41

4 PADDLING DUCKS AND TRANQUIL DUCKS:
Elegance and Self-Expression in Japan   64

5 BODY EFFICIENT:
The Japanese Culture of Movement   74

6 COMPACTED LIVING:
Command, Compliance, and Self-Realization   87

7 THE JAPANESE TAO OF STATUS   103

8 THE SELFLESS WAY TO SELFISHNESS:
Social Influence, Gift Giving, and Doing Favors   111

9 THE MIRROR AS FRIEND:
Japanese Intimacy and Affinity   123

10 NEVER GOOD ENOUGH:
The Japanese Addiction to Perfection and
Impossible Dreams   134

11 JAPANESENESS   147

12 EVALUATING JAPAN AND THE JAPANESE:
The Quality of the People, Society, and Culture   163

13 THE AUM SHINRIKYŌ AFFAIR,
THE JAPANESE NATIONAL CHARACTER,
AND THE FUTURE OF JAPANESE SOCIETY   179

Bibliography   197
Index   204

Acknowledgments

I have been fortunate to have had Japanese friends with a curiosity about their culture equal to mine. Over the years we have enjoyed long, exploratory talks, often far into the night. The most formative period for the development of my ideas was the early 1970s, and I acknowledge with gratitude the many talks with Masako and Masafumi Miyauchi and their friends, Ken and "Tong" Yajima, Fumie and Tatsuo Yamashita, and Kiyoshi Aonuma. During the past three to four years, as the idea of this book developed, I benefitted from discussions with Tatsuo and Keiko Kinugasa, Kengo Harada, Hideko Sato, Yasutaka Sai, and especially my youngest son, Gordon, whose insights into and deep knowledge of Japan's history and language, as well as his fine cultural sensitivity, are stimulating and exceptional. During 1995, Keiko Kinugasa and Diane Sasaki kindly collected press and video clips of reports and documentaries on Aum Shinrikyō, and my wife Anna has helped in many ways during the book's gestation. I thank them warmly.

Introduction

To understand another people, we must first understand ourselves. Westerners who would understand the Japanese must first grapple with and discover who they are themselves, what it is that makes them "Westerners," "Americans," "Europeans," or whatever.

If you were raised in a Western country, you are likely to know at least intuitively that the essence of Western civilization is *individualism*: the ideal that men and women are most naturally themselves when they speak their minds freely, form independent judgments, and pursue truth bravely, free of social pressure. It is a noble ideal.

The Japanese and Japanese culture know nothing of the sort. For them, the ideal of individualism is unnoble, risky. It shows a lack of common sense. The Japanese ideal portrays men and women behaving modestly, speaking prudently, and avoiding offense to others. It too is a noble ideal, but is, in its sensitivity to society and other people, individualism's antithesis.

While the Japanese desire people to be polite, courteous, and mildly self-deprecatory with one another, Westerners embrace a much more socially forthright model, where people feel unintimidated and comfortable with others, and speak their minds freely and frankly. The Japanese, reserving frankness for rarer occasions, strive to put the best "face" on themselves and situations, for to express what one really thinks or feels in Japan is regarded as uncultivated and gross.

If Japanese are a people truly alien to the West, how can they be

9

understood? If they are so formal, cautious, and prudent, preternaturally sensitive to what others think, trained from infancy to be courteous, polite, and hospitable, not letting on for a moment if they are disinterested, annoyed, or disheartened, are they not a closed book to Westerners? It is my task here to open the "book" on who the Japanese are, taking the reader on a journey into the many mansions of their inner lives and inner culture. Drawing on my life and experiences in Japan since first arriving in 1946, I tap into the rich body of knowledge about contemporary Japanese life, society, and psychology. My goal is to reveal the Japanese as they are at the end of the twentieth century, and especially to show that they are quite a different people to those defeated in 1945. In doing this, of course, I also draw upon what I have personally experienced and learned (usually from the Japanese themselves) over the years.

The task of reading the Japanese mind can only begin when we accept that we are all human in the end. Whatever the appearances might be (and there is no disputing that many non-Japanese have found some Japanese behavior in peace and war to be odd, perverse, or worse), Westerners and Japanese share and understand the highs and lows of human existence. Even if Japanese remained silent, we, by putting ourselves into their shoes and drawing on our common humanity, would not always find understanding them difficult. Certainly, their reputed "inscrutability" is no more than skin deep. Moreover, since World War II, Westerners and Japanese have steadily moved closer to one another, thanks to the Japanese "Peace Constitution" and increasing affluence. Higher education, living in nuclear families, significant amounts of leisure time, and individual rights are all taken for granted in the postwar world. Japanese men have lost much of their family authority and the stern masculinity that were de rigueur before the war. While once truly feared, they are now often emasculated figures of fun to their children. Likewise, women have lost much of their submissiveness and meek acceptance of their "inferiority." They are well educated, and their social status and work opportunities are slowly increasing. With the shift from agricultural to industrial/commercial workplaces and a more deliberately rational lifestyle, people are more worldly and less superstitious.

As a group-oriented people par excellence, the Japanese still stand in stark contrast to Westerners, however. They see themselves not in the first place as individuals, but as members of groups to which they have allegiances and responsibilities. They are preeminently social beings dependent on groups for approval, companionship, and identity. Growing up, they learn that the price of social acceptance is behaving as good girls or boys, following the social rules, and behaving with propriety. In adult life, this upbringing leads to a far greater striving for status and position at every level of society, to more submissive, service-oriented, self-sacrificing behavior than is conceivable in the West. This underlies a powerful national psychology of face, role playing, and indirect expression, and a general belief in the cultural superiority of Japan and the "spiritual" superiority of the Japanese people.

The social group gives identity, meaning, status, and surrogate kinship to the Japanese. How to describe this succinctly has long intrigued Japanese thinkers. Chie Nakane (1970) saw this rich set of meanings as providing a "frame" for each organizational member. In setting off the members of one group from all other groups, it provides a social identity that is not otherwise attainable in a society like Japan. Jun'ichi Mizuno (1984) disagreed. He called Japanese society a *maru* (circle) society, because "Japanese seek for unanimous approval wherever possible." The circle, he stated, is a Japanese "symbol of peace, OK, money, safe return, endlessness, or anything good." In consensual decision making, everyone from the highest to the lowest is involved. When proposals are approved by consensus, the Japanese often say *"Maruku osamatta"* (it has been settled in a fully rounded way). Michihiro Matsumoto (1978) used a food model of human relations in Japan, calling it a *nattō* (fermented soybeans) society. In *nattō* form, the beans sit in a sticky glue of starch, and it is not possible to extract one without also pulling out others that are connected by the same skeins of gluey starch. This, according to Matsumoto, represents the closeness and sticky togetherness of the Japanese. I imagine that Matsumoto would view individualistic Western societies as baked (canned) beans, which can easily be detached and eaten one at a time.

All of these easily grasped analogies reflect important aspects of Japanese society and culture, but my interest is in representing Japanese society generally, and for that the most powerful analogy is the box, that is, a frame with the extra dimension of depth. Box and frame are similar in suggesting that the contents all have a firm boundary, but the box has connotations of a more concrete reality. It emphasizes personal and spatial order, the avoidance of waste, the efficient use of space, as well as a general preference for the miniature and compact. O-Young Lee (1982), in his definitive book on the miniaturizing traditions of Japan, *Smaller Is Better*, showed that compacting by the Japanese has usually been done in boxes, as in the *bentō* (lunch box), created in feudal times by compressing a multicourse meal into the small space of a portable box. Many images of Japan, including dolls' houses, rabbit hutches, transistor radios, and *bentō*, are boxes. The Japanese do not have any special genius for working in large areas or on large concepts, but their genius flowers when working in small, precisely defined, compartmentalized areas.

If Japanese society is one great box, the groups and organizations within it are also boxes within or contiguous to other boxes. The chart opposite lists the characteristics that I believe are common to living in Japan and living in a box, or a dense, highly cohesive society. Box people see their society as secure, ordered, and relatively inert, and practice compression and compartmentalization in every aspect of their lives. They are trained from birth to be "social box animals," and to work and be productive within small frameworks and spaces.

In contrast, a society like the United States is neither boxlike nor compressed. It is the opposite of compact. The revolutionary tradition that sets the sturdy individualist "agin" the capitol makes commonplace antagonisms between government and business, between centralized control on the one hand and regional autonomy or individual autonomy (and rights) on the other. However we view it, the United States and some other Western countries tilt toward looser, more decentralized structures and perhaps more potential for social disintegration (or at least greater social diversity and plurality), and thus are antitheses of Japan. Instead of compression, in the West there is more expression, hyperbole, and rhetoric. Americans go down with a grand soliloquy; Japanese go down with quiet masochism.

SIMILARITIES BETWEEN LIVING IN JAPAN AND LIVING IN A BOX

* Life in a box or compartmentalized society means that great familiarity prevails.

* People know what others think about many matters, and the extent of interpersonal communication is reduced.

* Privacy is minimal.

* People believe that a society in harmony is possible (and essential) in small spaces.

* Manners, customs, rituals, methods of communication, etc., are standardized and routinized to enable everyone to look good and protect their face and honor in order to sustain the "harmonious society."

* People learn to fit in with everyone else by suppressing aggression.

* Dependence upon the identity developed within the restriction of four walls is overwhelming.

* People believe that this is the only world and there is nowhere to escape to.

* The exact coordinates of the box are used to make efficiency, precision, status ranking, space saving, compacting, economy, waste avoidance, etc., a way of life.

* The control and organization of life in the box induce a strong sense of order and security.

Specialization and professionalism, trademarks of American culture, are the antitheses of the multiskilling so dominant in Japan. American specialists consider they are doing their job when they promote professionalism first rather than organizational interests, even if that leads to confrontation between the center and the periphery, or the specific and the general. But specialists are almost anathema in Japan's industrial/business society. It is the generalist, à la general manager (= the multiskilled manager), who is dominant.

Westerners find much to praise and enjoy in Japan's compacted society: the people are polite, dedicated to getting along well with others, friendly, generous and hospitable, honest, sincere, and diligent. But there are also demerits, stemming from life in a dense, coherence-oriented society. For example, Westerners who know the Japanese well tend to say that they can be chauvinistic, cliquish, pushy, rude, submissive, close-minded, overorganized, not frank or open, unassertive, introverted, and uncomfortable with strangers. There is also another way to look at the Japanese, by listing expressions that are rarely used to describe them. That is, we could not describe the Japanese as extroverted, fun loving, independent-minded, individualistic, lighthearted, confident, optimistic, natural, open-minded, or outspoken. The lack of these qualities stems from the compactness of Japanese society.

The everyday closeness and interdependence of people, colored by traditions of Confucian vertically respectful behavior inside a compartmentalized world, make the Japanese different from Westerners. Moreover, many Japanese themselves are not slow to state that their fellow nationals "lack principle." Few have said this more incisively than the eminent political scientist Jun'ichi Kyogoku. In Japan, he reported, "There is no moral restraint against the corruption of power. There is no ethic based on moral commandments laid down by a transcendent creator-god ... [nor any] justification ... for demanding that those in power practice self-reflection and self-restraint...."

From an outsider's perspective, the succession of cases involving corruption in high places, including the Lockheed, Recruit, and Sagawa scandals, Toshiba planing machine exports to the former Soviet Union, the downfall of former Prime Minister Noboru Takeshita and political kingmaker Shin Kanemaru, indicates that corruption is widespread in politics and business. However, to the ordinary people of Japan, the high-level corruption in their own country is appalling, with no parallel in their own lives. That corruption of this kind does not run rampant throughout Japanese society, Kyogoku put down to "secular pragmatism." But there is much more to it than that. Other ethics prevail in potentially corrupting situations in Japan. One of Buddhist origin stresses, for example, that individuals who encounter one another in everyday life are fulfilling karmic inevitabilities and should therefore show compassion to one another. There are ethics of familism and paternalism, originating in Confucianism, which insist that seniors should care for juniors in a paternalistic or avuncular manner. Ethics related to gift giving and the return of favors also partly put restrictions upon the size of gifts or returns of favors.

STRUCTURE OF THE BOOK

The aim of this book is to create an understanding of Japan and the Japanese people today, by examining their business and personal behavior. I write as someone who lived in Japan on and off between 1946 and 1988, a period of extraordinary change. My first years in Japan covered the immediate postwar period, when in many ways Japan was still a feudal society. From 1970 to 1988, I lived and worked in Tokyo, Kobe, Fujinomiya, and Nishinomiya as a management consultant, business professor, professional psychologist, and an "ordinary" taxpayer and resident with an overweening curiosity about Japan. The Japan I know is and always has been a "dense," "boxed-up," group-oriented society, very much unlike the one I was born into. Its members feel close to, familiar, and comfortable with one another, but often uncomfortable, uneasy with, and estranged from, me and other Caucasian foreigners.

To adapt successfully to Japanese society, one needs to acquire an exceptionally wide range of social and communication skills. In the social background, there is also a unique social, historical, and geographical framework that affects every member. In describing a culture with its own special rules for the achievement of largely trouble-free, well-adjusted lives, the first four chapters look at Japanese social and communication behavior, and at particular ways of thinking which differ from those in Western societies.

On a different dimension, how people use their bodies is regarded by some scholars as the most clear-cut sign of what a culture is all about. This is certainly true of the Japanese. The restraint that is such a feature of Japanese culture is in the first place a restraint of the body and of physical movement, as seen in their pokerface and capacity for being still. Chapter 5 shows that how the Japanese use their bodies is a window on the culture. In an understanding of Japanese body movement lies the secrets of their manual dexterity and expressive nonverbal behavior, as they compress their bodies to achieve emotional and physical precision and control.

Chapters 6 and 7 examine the nature of the social, group, and organizational framework that is the bearer from generation to generation of the constantly changing cultural heritage. In terms of what individual Japanese learn of their society, it is as inheritors of this "framework" that they become inculcated with their cultural values.

Having learned how to behave socially and physically, and having become an adept member of the culture, a young Japanese can at length begin to feel confident that he/she can move up in the world, acquire status, and become "someone." But the quest for status differs in many ways from that in the West. The values of the culture insist that people should be selfless and work for the good of society. This pervasive ethic inhibits the overt behavior of even the most fiercely ambitious. It is responsible for the fact that financial rewards for Japanese in high positions are much more modest than those in the West, and that income differentials are smaller than in any other advanced country. The Japanese rich and famous consume less conspicuously and are less ostentatious than their counterparts in the West. More important by far are the status and respect assigned by others. Connected to selflessness and status striving are gift giving, doing favors, and the creation and repayment of obligations. Occasionally these go beyond everyday ethics into the realms of bribery and corruption. Chapter 8 explains the issues involved.

Chapter 9 examines the key factors of appearance and personality in others that are most attractive or unattractive to the Japanese. These are the bases of affinity between Japanese and non-Japanese. The chapter says much that is new about the barriers that impede affinity between foreigners and Japanese. Understanding what fosters affinity is the beginning of genuine long-term intimacy in human relations with the Japanese.

Japanese economic successes owe much to the "addiction" of the Japanese people to perfection in small things, and to that idealizing and visionary part of their minds that often drives them to realize sometimes impossible dreams. But, as Chapter 10 shows, suggestibility and gullibility are exceptionally common as well, and may be essential to the disciplined behavior that underlies postwar economic success.

In Chapter 11, I look closely at deeper levels of Japanese culture which help make sense of what it means to be Japanese. Two aspects of national psychology, powerful attachments to the country, its people, and its institutions, and the sense of uniqueness that springs particularly from their sense of difference from Westerners, are shown to be the sources of much of the energy and powerful emotionality that lie beneath the surface of everyday restraint.

Chapter 12 looks at the question of how "good" a society Japan is. This is a pertinent question for Americans. As Karl Greenfield (1991) wrote in *The Nation*, when commenting on Michael Crichton's novel *Rising Sun*: "Crichton has brought to the surface an idea that has been lurking for some years in America's collective pop-unconscious: the Japanese are evil." Are they "evil" in any sense? Such a question cannot be answered subjectively, or by reference to "good" American values. To compare Japanese with American culture, or any others, we need to assess both according to *universal* criteria—values, social structures, and human models that best serve humankind. The evaluation of Japan in the light of universal values is the point of Chapter 12.

Chapter 13, the final chapter, was added after the first twelve chapters had been completed. It analyzes the impact on Japanese society of the sarin gas attacks and revelations about the religious cult Aum Shinrikyo. This analysis adds significantly to our understanding of the Japanese people and their urban culture fifty years after the end of World War II.

SOCIAL MAN, *TATEMAE* MAN

The first lesson in understanding the Japanese is to recognize that "things" are not as they appear, words may not mean what they seem to mean, and appearance can be more important than "truth." The keys to this understanding are the way Japanese use "face" and tatemae.

Harunobu Kawasaki is a director of an overseas subsidiary of Canon Incorporated, the camera and office automation products giant. "Call me Hal," he says when abroad. He is a friendly, decent human being. Four local English-speaking managers report to Hal, and because his English is by no means perfect, he faces daily problems of communication in the process of managing effectively. Some of his problems are readily understandable. For instance, a manager who promised to finish a certain project by a specific date did not meet the deadline. Hal in turn had promised his president that it would be completed, and he has been let down. "Why wasn't the project finished on time?" Hal asked. The local manager launched into a long explanation, and soon Hal lost the gist of what he was being told. The manager's speech was too quick and too colloquial. But Hal continued to nod, as though he understood. When Hal finally ended the meeting, the local manager still did not realize that Hal had not understood the explanation.

Another type of problem is less understandable, at least to the Western mind. One of his managers submitted an innovative recommendation for the reorganization of the division, which had obviously taken a lot of time to prepare. To Hal, as to most Japanese managers, an innovative proposal affecting the jobs and interests of others should be first thoroughly discussed with those people and their views taken into account before the proposal is submitted to management. But the local manager did not discuss his recommendations with anyone. Hal, not knowing what to do with such an un-Japanese proposal, could only pigeonhole it. A few weeks later, the local manager asked Hal if he had had a chance to read the proposal. Hal gave an equivocal answer, saying neutrally that he had taken a brief look at it. The manager waited for Hal to say more, and when he did not inquired if Hal could give him any feedback about the proposal. Hal replied that he would really need to look at it again. The local manager, disappointed that Hal was telling him nothing, walked crestfallen from the room.

GRASPING THE UNSTATED

If Hal had been dealing with another Japanese in the above situations, he would have assumed that the manager really knew that he did not understand what was being said in the former case, and that he was not interested in the proposal in the latter case. A Japanese who did not intuitively understand what Hal was really thinking would in fact be regarded by Hal and most other Japanese managers as "an unpromotable idiot." On the face of it and looking purely at the words used, people behaving like Hal might be thought to be agreeing to something, or at least indicating "nondenial." But words in themselves in Japan are not the message. It is a society where, in the office or the coffee shop or the bar, communication is indirect, built upon hints and nonverbal cues. If, in spite of signs obvious to Japanese of what one was thinking or feeling— especially the absence of enthusiasm and the choice of neutrally toned words—a subordinate did not "cotton on" to the real message, he would be unable to survive as an effective member of a work-oriented group.

TATEMAE *MAKES THE JAPANESE WORLD GO ROUND*

The Japanese have a word to describe overt behavior, especially verbal behavior, that is deliberately contrary to what one is really feeling: *tatemae*. *Tatemae* can be thought of as the most important social lubricant in Japan. It is the gentle substitute for the harsh words one might be thinking, or for the refusal or disagreement that would hurt or offend if put bluntly. *Tatemae* makes the Japanese world go round and includes putting on a good face, white lies, making the unpalatable a little more palatable, avoiding trouble, and dressing things up nicely for public consumption. It is said in Japan that the citizens of different countries vary in their ability to understand what *tatemae* is. Americans must be given a detailed explanation in advance, otherwise they will not see through it. The Chinese understand it at once. The English soon see through it, while the French know from the beginning that everything is *tatemae*.

A FINE ART

Tatemae is practiced by human beings everywhere, but the Japanese have raised it to a fine art. In the midst of an everyday life that is already characterized by degrees of civilities, courtesies, and elegant understatements unknown elsewhere, *tatemae* fits the conflict-avoiding Japanese society to a tee. It is not merely a pragmatic set of customs, but an essential part of the ethical system and the bulwark of everyday morality in Japanese society. The way that Hal acted was based on what he feels most strongly is proper behavior and is second nature to a Japanese, instinctive, and needing no reflection.

   Tatemae is mandatory for a Japanese in dealings with visitors and superiors. Educated, cultivated Japanese are taught to believe in and practice the Zen axiom *"Ichigo ichie,"* which advocates regarding each time a guest is received as though it were only to occur once in a lifetime, so that one should strive to make it a perfect occasion. Among other things, this means doing and saying whatever will make the guest feel honored and important; in other words, practicing *tatemae*, but *tatemae* at its very best and most elegant. Pleasing words to superiors are also important. As superiors, the Japanese believe, they deserve flattery, and subordinates are viewed as serving well when they voice such flattery.

TATEMAE *CAN CONFUSE*

Among the Japanese, it is understood that words can just be words on certain occasions, and nothing further is expected. Westerners dealing with the Japanese, however, need to understand the situational nature of *tatemae* if they are to avoid misunderstandings, confusion, and possibly worse. While it lubricates social relationships among the Japanese, non-Japanese usually have reactions that the Japanese do not anticipate. *Tatemae* behavior can puzzle and generate misunderstandings and unintended expectations, especially when words taken as a promise turn out not to be a promise at all, thus undermining trust.

Suppose, for example, that you are meeting a group of Japanese for the first time to explore the possibility of a business relationship. They entertain you royally and impress you mightily with their organization. In everything they say, they convey their ability to make extraordinary efforts. But should you believe them? This is a matter requiring delicate consideration. At this early stage in your discussions, what you should believe at most is that they are interested in having a relationship with you—some time, somewhere, not necessarily immediately or related to the subject you have raised. But you should not take the nice things they have said, or the seeming "promises" they have made, at face value. You should take them, as a Japanese in your position would, as *tatemae*.

Slogans are used frequently in most countries, embodying

statements of intent or belief assumed to be held by all citizens, or encouraging citizens to take certain action. Those used in Japan (as well as in China and Korea), however, have special qualities. Often highly melodramatic, their merit lies more in the sentiment under-lying them than in whether individuals actually identify with them. At the start of the Pacific War, the slogan "*Ichioku isshin*" (one hundred million people, one heart) was promoted throughout the Japanese empire. The implication was that everyone was united into one vast, close, single-minded family. Many disagreed pri-vately with this, but the truth of the matter to the Japanese was the sentiment, not the principle. Toward the end of the war, when inva-sion was imminent, a new slogan emerged: "*Ichioku gyokusai*" (one hundred million honorable deaths), meaning that, rather than surrender to or be captured by the Americans, everyone should either die in battle or by his own hand. The sentiment was admirable to the Japanese, even though few contemplated death or suicide.

Soon after the war finished, and only weeks after the honorable death slogan was promulgated, a new slogan, "*Ichioku sō zange*" (one hundred million repentances), spread like wildfire. Once again, this was *tatemae*, a statement of sentiment concerning what appeared to be appropriate behavior in the face of the conquerors. Again, while a few felt repentant, mainly residents and officials in the capital, especially if they spoke English, most Japanese were largely indifferent.

Tatemae slogans continue to be earnestly advocated and repeated in speeches, talks, and articles by politicians, commenta-tors, and academics. Recent slogans have concerned "international-ization" of the country and the people, globalization of enterprises, the importance of the Self-Defense Forces, decentralization (of business and government offices from Tokyo to the prefectures), the restoration of political ethics, and so on. A good test of whether these are *tatemae* or not is what substantive discussions have occurred about the meaning of the key terms. Regrettably, most sloganeering in Japan, as elsewhere, fails the test. In Japan, there is no climate favoring the discussion or analysis of what such key words or slogans really mean, because it is sufficient if the slogan appeals to a nice but semantically cloudy sentiment. As long as Japanese tarry, as they are wont to, at the sentimental level of words and slogans, it is easy to hold seemingly contradictory *tatemae* views with no sense of intellectual dissonance. This is a feature of the Japanese way of thinking examined more closely in Chapter 3.

TATEMAE, *SECRETIVENESS, AND FACE*

Karel van Wolferen, a well-known writer on Japan, has called *tatemae* "socially sanctioned deceit." Given Western values, this is understandable. Some *tatemae* is indeed used to feign emotions that do not exist. Feigning contrition and sorrow is extremely common. The daily volume of self-humbling penitences, metaphorical knee-bending, and commiserating is huge, from children apologizing glibly to parents, teachers, and seniors, to adult conversation richly spiced with "sorry" and "excuse me," relating as much to things that have happened in the past or will happen in the future as to the present. Much is precautionary (just to be on the safe side in case one offends in the future), demonstrating that, whatever one did or will say, "I am on your side and my heart is in the right place." Many Westerners feel it to be excessive and a little distasteful, even servile and hypocritical. But the Japanese perception should not be misunderstood. *Tatemae* of the kind I have been discussing is a part of good manners and proper civilities in Japan. There is a big difference between *tatemae* that stems from a sense of courtesy and is appropriate to be used with others in the same cultural domain, and "hypocritical politeness" (which the Japanese are keenly aware of).

Inevitably, at a deeper level *tatemae* is also about being secretive, or hiding things that ought not to be revealed to outsiders. Comments critical of one's company, for instance, can never be made in public. Nor can information, especially of a strategic nature, about the company be revealed. Therefore, to preserve face, *tatemae* statements are substituted: things that are not nice are given pretty names, flowery words are used about people one cares little for, poses are struck, and egos are professionally massaged. But underneath all this, many individual Japanese remain, by Western standards, particularly secretive people. The culture has long advocated secrecy. In feudal times, a merchant's ways of doing business, the recipes of a restaurant, the techniques of a craftsman, and so on were all regarded as proprietary, secret information not to be passed on to others. The expression *"isshi sōden"* means the transmitting of trade secrets from a father to a son, and this continues even today, especially in traditional industries and crafts. Secrecy, discretion, and maintaining confidences are still normative in Japan. Japanese keep daily diaries as a part of their required assignments from elementary school, usually writing the most mundane of entries when young, but when older sometimes recording the most intimate details, and keeping the diary itself under lock and key.

Secretiveness is regarded as proper behavior because it is assumed that unspecified others could steal one's trade or other secrets and profit from them, thereby damaging one's own business. In 1970, a Japanese friend kindly searched for an apartment for me in the city of Kobe. When she had found a satisfactory one, she told the realtor that a foreigner would reside in it. In those days, realtors and landlords had had so little experience of foreigners that the "no foreigners" rule had not yet been formulated in the Kansai region. But the realtor was curious, and asked what sort of a person the foreigner was. When told that he was an academic doing research on Japanese business, his eyes narrowed. "Is he coming to steal all our secrets?" he queried, with a mixture of distaste and suspicion.

A business relationship between two Japanese, however long it endures, will usually be characterized by extreme discretion, reserve, and guardedness on both sides. Even close business or professional friends in Japan know amazingly little about the personal or family lives of one another. Part of this is due, management consultant Kazuo Nomura told me, to the fact that young Japanese businessmen, in their first ten or so years in a company, cannot say what they really think. "They must hold themselves back and tell themselves lies in order to survive," Nomura explains. In my own experience, a great many young businessmen have confided bitterly, "Japanese business is 99 percent *tatemae*. You cannot say what you really think." And unfortunately, by the time young men have reached management level, this way of operating may have become habitual, with their capacity to speak up and make innovative proposals inhibited and crippled.

A book could be written about another type of secretiveness in Japan, namely, taboos. The central force behind the keeping of many taboos in Japanese society is the Imperial Household Agency. Responsible in particular for the personal, ceremonial, and official affairs of the Emperor and his family, and for imperial tombs, it is a secretive, greatly feared agency that operates from the shadows to suppress, so far successfully, public information about the imperial family and its members. In fact, writers, publishers, and the media in Japan accept these taboos. They have a tacit agreement to make no personal comments about the imperial family, which is coincidentally reinforced by the real threat of violence, or even assassination, from extreme right-wing groups and *yakuza* (gangsters). When writing my first book in Japanese in 1986, I was forced by my publisher to delete a chapter on then Crown Princess Michiko, which traced extraordinary changes in her posture from the time she became engaged to the Crown Prince. The changes were massive, from a fluid, relaxed, well-balanced posture in 1955 to a permanently out-of-balance upper body in 1985, and I suggested that these could be attributed to long-term hazing she had reportedly endured from her mother-in-law, the Dowager Empress. It is only recently that media reports about the tough apprenticeship that Michiko underwent have begun to appear.

The Imperial Household Agency is heavily criticized by

archaeologists and others for its refusal to allow the largest of all the imperial tombs, that of the fifth-century Emperor Nintoku, to be excavated or studied by scholars. Since the agency has given no explanation for its refusal, the commonest speculation is that it fears that the tomb may contain clear evidence that the Emperor Nintoku was Korean, which would deal a death blow to much of Japanese mythology about the origins of Japan, and inflict a devastating loss of face on the nation.

Very recently, there have been frankly scandalous rumors about the private lives of the Emperor and his family, at least on a par with what has emerged about the British royal family. I do not have the courage to reveal here what I have been told (always in hushed whispers after a comprehensive inspection of the surroundings to ensure that no one can overhear) by excellent sources, because I would frankly fear something unpleasant happening to me, my family, or the publisher. Almost every Japanese will understand my feelings, for they are how any Japanese would feel in the circumstances, and as long as *yakuza* and extreme right wingers retain the power that they have in Japan, it is hard to imagine scandalous or horrific stories about the imperial family being made public.

On the other hand, the whole public mood about another once-taboo subject in Japan has changed significantly in the past ten years. This is industrial espionage. Ten years ago, I researched an article on how the war strategies of Sun Tzu were accepted in Japan. A key axiom of Sun Tzu is "Deception is the way of the warrior," which seems to be a perfect justification of espionage (of any type). My Japanese business respondents at that time either pooh-poohed the idea that industrial espionage existed in Japan, or warned that this was not something one talked about because the subject was so "dirty" or "dishonorable" that it was deeply objectionable even to discuss it or ask questions. But times change, the trade in industrial secrets is finally being exposed, and it is now possible to receive introductions to "consultants" in Japan who specialize in obtaining and selling this sort of information.

FACE AND TATEMAE

Face is akin to the concept of *tatemae*. The Japanese have a saying, "When you reach thirty, be responsible for what you say. When you reach forty, be responsible for your face." This face one is responsible for covers many things: honor, appearance of propriety, presence, and impact on others. Taking responsibility for one's face means taking responsibility for and controlling what is expressed facially or by external appearance, as well as the effect one produces on others.

What Face Means to Japanese

Putting on a face (which is a form of *tatemae*) means concealing or at least prettying-up what you are really feeling. The Japanese are very sophisticated about the matter of face or appearance versus reality. While they take great pains to ensure that their own and others' faces are not "lost," they are also aware of hypocritical behavior. Japanese sophistication about face can be appreciated by considering one of the commonest expressions used in Japanese business: "Deferential to his face, but abusive behind his back." A "face friend" to the Japanese is, unsurprisingly, a "fair-weather friend." But face is not always sacrosanct, even among the Japanese. Another common proverb says, "Tear off the surface face." This is used when it is felt that some persons ought not to have their faces protected, and that it is acceptable or necessary for them to be attacked and exposed for the scoundrels they presumably are. The Japanese also say, "Look at both sides of the shield!" In other words, do not look only at the lustrous and splendid face of things, but also at the back, which might be quite different.

Limits of face

A sense of the sometimes illusory nature of reality and the ambiguity of things is central to the formation of business relationships in

Japan. Face and *tatemae* are important in lubricating superficial or ongoing contacts, but there are also limits to the faith put in face alone which Westerners need to understand. The expressions "*Hana yori dango*" (dumplings before flowers), and "*Ron yori shōko*" (evidence, not theory) are representative of what most Japanese businesspeople regard as the heart of practical wisdom. Ultimately, they indicate that substance, content, and reality are important. One cannot eat flowers, rely on appearances, or survive on theories.

STYLE AND TATEMAE

Deeply ingrained in Japanese culture is the emphasis on putting on one's best face in formal situations. The practice was already ancient in the seventeenth century when samurai were enjoined to appear at their very best, in their best armor, freshly washed and shaven, when venturing abroad or meeting an enemy. It was expected that they would spend hours preparing themselves, even using a pumice stone to rub away any hairs appearing on the shaven area of their heads. One of the most flattering things a man can be called today is "a dandy" (using the Japanized word *dandi*, or the older word *oshare*). I am not sure how many young Japanese today realize it, but *oshare* in former times were men who spent much of their time being dandies in the licensed prostitution areas. The word *dandi* came into Japanese much later. Amusingly, when the movie *Crocodile Dundee* was shown in Japan, in the title transliteration the word *Dundee* became "dandy." Many Japanese thus thought Paul Hogan was some mutant dandy from the Australian bush, and warmed to the anomalous antipodean character even more.

THE BEST OF TATEMAE *AND FACE*

In its best sense, *tatemae* is used to maintain good human relationships and avoid trouble in a society hinged upon a well-voiced philosophy of harmony and goodwill. To do otherwise, to the extent of brutally calling a spade a spade, is effectively antisocial behavior in Japan. The Japanese are exceptionally sensitive to criticism and rebuffs, and have an open conspiracy to ensure that others as well as themselves are protected and shielded from psychological injury. It is proper behavior to say only good things about others, and to have nothing ill to say about one's own team or colleagues. To maintain a good tone (the right sentiment) in human relations, *tatemae* extends to apologies and feigning sincerity and contrition.

When a business relationship is established and becomes ongoing, then preserving the face of one's associates and colleagues (foreign or Japanese) becomes a very important part of the give and take, the favors received, and the favors given. Business discussions, the protocol of Japanese social intercourse insists, should be conducted in a way that offends no one. This is the ever-open door through which *tatemae*—the always artful construction of a quasireality that offends none but communicates volumes to the initiate—is invited again and again into the world of Japanese business relationships.

To summarize, Japanese culture has a very sophisticated set of values concerning the appearance and reality of things. On the surface, it is a world of illusion and ambiguity, where only a fool would wear his heart on his sleeve, or display his shortcomings or defects for all to see. The oft-stated view that Japanese always strive to maintain face stems from an extreme sensitivity about one's personal defects, and the function of masks and faces is both to hide these and to promote the public honor of people or oneself. *Tatemae* can be thought of as a denial of defects, showing why *tatemae*-suffused communication is accepted so readily among the Japanese. As a non-Japanese involved in long-term relationships with the Japanese, one understands that there are times of "flowers" and times of "dumplings." Work at making the "flowers" of the relationship look elegant, beautiful, tasteful, and harmonious. Then, when practical, or "dumpling," issues are discussed, understand that face and *tatemae* have been put aside for a rational, issue-oriented approach. Those with the flexibility to change gears in relationships with the Japanese will most likely pierce the many barriers to effective business relationships.

Putting business relationships aside, what can we conclude about the use of face and *tatemae* in personal relationships? The only conclusion to reach is that face and *tatemae* reach the limits of their usefulness when relationships begin to move toward openness and intimacy. Unfortunately, there is so much concern among Japanese, especially younger people, about hiding their defects and avoiding criticism that many people become very skillful in using face and *tatemae* behavior, avoiding taboo subjects, using only polite, calculated language, and denying their own shortcomings to themselves as well as to others. The cost of this is that they deaden their own ability to distinguish, in themselves or others, between what is *tatemae* and what is the genuine thing.

2

YES MAY MEAN NO:
How the Japanese
Communicate

Verbal communication is far less important than other
forms to the Japanese. They live in a culture that fosters
elegant, standardized human interactions. Only in private
can we begin to communicate with the "real person."

How well do the Japanese communicate, with each other or with
non-Japanese? With a penchant for self-deprecation, most Japanese would say they communicate poorly with foreigners, but effectively among themselves. There are, they are likely to add, special
problems in communicating with foreigners: Japanese is too
difficult for foreigners to use properly; English too difficult for
Japanese. Such judgments reflect everyday experiences of problems
in communication with foreigners, in Japan or abroad.

Among themselves, the Japanese perceive few communication
problems, believing that they have perfected indirect, nonverbal
ways of communication that are efficient, sophisticated, and elegant.
Silence, indirect expressions, intuitive understanding, the use of
euphemisms, nonverbal language, and gestures, and the like, are
also regarded by the Japanese as esthetic acts, because they are
done with style to effect communication with the minimum of
words or effort.

THE ELEGANCE OF GESTURE

Living among the Japanese, I know that speech-minimizing behaviors are both elegant and efficient, and, like other foreigners who speak Japanese, I use them stylistically to communicate feelings or uncomplicated ideas. This ability to simplify is very important in Japan, because the speaker must be sure that the words chosen are appropriately respectful to the subject or the listener. Nonverbal communication such as gestures or euphemisms that do not directly "call a spade a spade" are socially "safer" for the Japanese to use and much "cleaner" because they lack the nuances and overtones of direct verbal reference that might give offense or lead to misunderstandings. Such nonverbal messages have an obvious economy, clarity, efficiency, and directness that words cannot achieve.

As examples of commonly used Japanese gestures, if the thumb and index finger are joined into a circle to represent a small saké cup, then tossed toward the mouth while looking at a friend across the room, this is an invitation to go for a drink. An upright thumb means man, or boss, or boyfriend, or husband; an upright little finger, woman, wife, or girlfriend. If someone sees a female friend talking to a man, an interested look, a raised eyebrow, and a raised thumb would be sufficient to inquire, "Was that your boyfriend?" This would be regarded as a much more delicate, elegant means of communication than a direct question. An equally elegant, not to say humorous, response could be a tilt of the head (signifying uncertainty in Japan) with a mysterious smile. Although this episode still leaves the inquirer wondering who the man was, it is emotionally complete and satisfying for the Japanese. The inquirer does not feel shut out as one might if the response had been verbal, for example, if one's friend had replied "no comment," implying that one was prying.

Many of my Japanese friends exhibit a similar inclination to an esthetically pleasing communication shorthand. One friend always answers the telephone with a mellifluous and assertive, "Chie!" This is her given name, uttered unconventionally, without the grammatically complete, "This is Chie," or the redundant and conventional, "Chie here." So she uses her name, most stylishly, like a signature to a letter or drawing.

If a latter-day Japanese Shakespeare were to write, "To communicate or not to communicate, that is the question," he would capture perfectly the intense Japanese consciousness of and concern about speech, silence, inquiry, questions, praise, and how others might perceive what one says or does not say: to inquire or not to inquire what is really being said; to question or not to question; to be silent or to speak; to praise or not to praise. To be Japanese is to be faced by these choices constantly and to lose innocence about what other people say. Japanese believe that what is heard is only a fraction of what is meant, the tip of the meaning iceberg.

How can one know what is really being said? Unless people are intimates and on the same status level, then the only way to know is by intuition, or asking others what a speaker really meant. Face to face with seniors or elders, a Japanese can only praise or be obedient. The traditional culture originating in Confucian China more than one thousand years ago does not permit juniors to question seniors. At some later point, intuitiveness was emphasized, giving rise to the general injunction widely accepted today that "questions are for fools." There are other, somewhat contradictory, proverbs, such as, "*Kiku wa ittoki no haji; kikanu wa matsudai no haji*" (to inquire is a moment of shame; not to inquire is a lasting shame). The avoidance of inquiry or questions, however, represents everyday common sense in modern Japan.

AVOIDING THE CATEGORICAL

Even in everyday verbal discourse, the Japanese tend to avoid categorical comments. If one Japanese asks another, "Are you tired?" the likely answer will be, "Not especially," or at most, "A little," but certainly not a forthright, "Yes, I am." The social point of this kind of behavior in Japan is to appear undemanding, flexible, or nonegotistical, all of which are desirable qualities. Asked to make choices, such as, "Will you have coffee or tea?" or "Will you eat or bathe first?" good manners in Japan dictate that first response should be, "Either is fine." The questioner is then likely to follow up with, "Which do you prefer?" so that the respondent is forced to make a choice. Everyone in Japan knows the rules of social interaction and customary language, and thus the system works well. But put Japanese with such social/language habits among foreigners, and things will not proceed as smoothly. Foreign flight attendants are baffled when, in response to the question, "Coffee or tea?" some Japanese passengers answer, "Either is fine."

Indirect expressions become sources of irritation in communication with foreigners. The Japanese have many ways of indicating "no," without actually saying so explicitly. "That will be difficult," and "I'll think about it" are common circumlocutions. Japanese who hear such statements have a pretty good idea that the answer is definitely "no," but non-Japanese usually interpret the word "difficult" literally, as meaning inability or incompetence. If a non-Japanese tries to assist the Japanese to solve apparent problems of inability or incompetence, confusion and misunderstanding can escalate quickly, for the apparent problems do not in fact exist. Being "difficult" is merely a Japanese euphemism for "impossible." Misunderstandings are also likely if a "think about it" response is taken literally as a promise to consider the matter.

JAPANESE PROBLEMS WITH WESTERN DIRECTNESS

Just as the foreigner can become confused when faced with Japanese indirectness, Japanese can become confused about Western directness, feeling that it must have some ulterior motive or meaning, as would likely be the case in Japan. An American writer friend, who worked from his suburban Tokyo home, was under heavy pressure to meet a deadline. Rather brusquely, he said to his Japanese wife, "The children are making too much noise. I can't concentrate. Take them to your mother's place, and don't come back until tonight." But the wife believed that the husband was actually telling her and the children to leave permanently, and did not return. It took some time for this particular misunderstanding to be clarified.

Western managers of foreign companies in Japan commonly experience problems of this kind. One English manager decided to award good work by a young Japanese woman staffer with a trip to the parent company office in London. He expected her to be pleased, but she remained stony-faced and showed no interest. After repeated questioning, she eventually said, "I know what you are really trying to do. You are just trying to create an obligation in me so that I will have to stay with this company." This seemingly paranoid reaction is certainly not typical in Japan, but it does illustrate how Japanese tend to look behind what they are told, in search of the "real meaning."

More common are cases like the following. A neighbor being kept awake at night by the young girl next door practicing her piano exclaims to the child's mother, "My goodness! I'm so impressed with the progress your daughter is making with her piano studies. It seems only yesterday she was doing scales. She's so conscientious about her practice as well, almost every night." In Japan, virtually everyone would recognize the real, underlying message at once, and the mother would reply immediately, "I am very sorry that she is such a nuisance, practicing late like that, without considering others. She will not do it again." Using indirect communication, the Japanese depend on the acuteness and sensitivity of the other person to pick up the real message, and therefore conflict is avoided.

Such indirectness and allusiveness indicate that the Japanese attitude to language is different to that in the West. Westerners are heirs to a tradition of intellectual debate and the search for truth that can ultimately be expressed in words. The Japanese tradition with roots in Zen Buddhism appears to be almost the opposite. The emphasis since ancient times has been upon immediate rather than "mediated" experience. Intellectually verbalized experience, which includes debate, theory, rhetoric, etc., is even today the major example of mediated experience to the Japanese. Daisetsu Suzuki, the great modern exponent of Zen, wrote (1959): "In the study of Zen, conceptualization must go; for as long as we tarry at this level we can never reach the area where Zen has its life."

Individual Japanese do not usually think in such terms, just as few Westerners think in terms of Greek concepts of individuality, but the cultural injunctions against excessive verbalizing still affect everyday behavior in Japan. The culture is rich in proverbs that decry words and talk. "Silence is golden," a meaningful proverb in the West three or four centuries ago, is still seen as relevant in Japan. One also commonly hears, "Talk is the root of trouble," "Keep your mouth closed and your eyes open," and occasionally even the old Chinese saying, "In your speech, honey; in your heart, a sword."

ORDERLY, ORGANIZED, STANDARDIZED LANGUAGE

Japan is still a hierarchical society, and the language is adapted to acknowledge the social status of the person being addressed. A central theme of Japanese society is "respect authority." Even if an individual believes authority is wrong, cultural values require a search for consensual, indirect ways of bringing change about, so that no one's face is lost. There is still no place in Japanese society for debate or argument, which is viewed as threatening to the harmonious status quo that hinges at every level upon respect for authority. The many standardized phrases that all Japanese expect to use and to be used in certain situations—getting up in the morning, leaving the house, seeing someone off, returning home, at the start of a meal, going to bed, arriving at and departing from the office, greeting guests, meeting old friends one has not seen for some time, etc.—are obviously aimed at preserving the status quo.

Unlike many Western countries, in Japan creative self-expression in conversation is neither aspired to nor welcomed. It is not even socially "safe," since unexpected expressions can be misunderstood, appear to lack courtesy, or seem ironic or even disparaging. With the plethora of standardized phrases, in some situations everything that is said is standardized. While other cultures make use of set phrases as well, they are so extensively developed and fluently used by the Japanese that it is common for non-Japanese to believe that what they are hearing springs from the heart. In fact they are merely standardized phrases, albeit gracious and often elegant in expression, even when translated into other languages.

Do not mistake this for hypocrisy, however. Using set phrases is a price paid to live effectively in any society; it just happens that Japan's compact society demands the use of many more. Although it may seem paradoxical, one should not underestimate the individuality of the Japanese. In their formal behavior they tend to follow conventions and present a standardized front, but in private life and informally, a large measure of style and individuality pervades their communication with others.

Given the standardized character of much conversation in Japan, it is not surprising that the Japanese themselves do not feel they learn much from what others say. If everyone is set on eliminating everything controversial, arguable, or challenging from what they say, then often no one communicates much except for harmony-reinforcing "stroking" that reinforces good feelings between people. Once foreigners who deal with Japanese learn to appreciate this, they also gain insight into what it is like to be Japanese: to have no idea, based on what others say, of what they are really thinking. This is a major, inevitable consequence of the culture's emphasis upon respecting seniors, and being polite, undemanding, flexible, and nonegotistical.

COMMUNICATION PROBLEMS IN JAPAN

As in other advanced countries, many Japanese suffer from interpersonal communication problems. Dr. Sui Shibata runs a Tokyo clinic to treat such people and views problems of relating to others as major and disabling for Japanese. They usually try to solve them by culturally conventional, nonverbal means—what he calls "heart-to-heart connection" and "attitude." Japanese expect these to lead to "intimate familiarity." Shibata points out that foreigners find these Japanese ways of, in his words, "trying to touch each other's core," baffling, because they seem so insubstantial, vague, and illogical. On the other hand, Japanese culture teaches that "heart-to-heart communication" comes first and cannot be achieved logically. It is confusing and painful, Shibata adds, for so many Japanese to find that upon first meeting both Japanese and foreigners begin by being dry and logical. This seems almost inhuman, the Japanese feel, and think secretly to themselves, "Why doesn't this person realize that the process of getting comfortable with others begins with the heart and not the head?"

The following passage of dialogue from the transcript of US-Japan business negotiations (McCreary, 1986) is probably a typical exchange:

Japanese: Have you visited Tokyo?
American: We really haven't had any time yet to see anything. I thought we'd open with the letter of the twenty-third.

Thereafter it is all business until the American makes a request.

American: Do you mind if I smoke?
Japanese: OK.
American: By the way [extending his right hand], I'm Ed. This is Walter.
Walter: Hi.
American: We might as well call each other by first names.
Interpreter: It won't be easy to call you by your first names. This is not a Japanese custom. Please call us by our last names.
American: Is there a reason for that? It's not always easy to do that.

Both the Japanese and Americans are ill at ease here; neither side understands the other. The Americans' lack of ease prevented them from engaging in initial nonbusiness conversation, while the cold, "let's get down to business" opening of the Americans was probably unfamiliar to the Japanese.

How do the Japanese keep in touch with what others are really thinking and feeling, or with what is going on in their world? Some Japanese would answer that all that is necessary is to know what one is required to do. In a Japanese organization, this often means that one merely waits to be "tapped on the shoulder" by one's superiors. This is the orientation of people happy to be followers, whose greatest pleasures lie in the security of their job, the patronage of their boss, and the certainty of support from social connections or intimate friends.

Many Japanese, however, are more than camp followers. They are thinkers who will speak their minds to Japanese or non-Japanese friends. This is especially the case when they are professionals or independent people who do not belong to large organizations. Many of my Japanese friends fit this category (including lawyers, architects, writers, educators, and accountants), and each has original, perceptive things to say, although one might not believe that when meeting them formally. On the surface, they would probably look and act just like other Japanese: neat, standardized human "products" from a country famous for its fine mass-produced products. They are living testaments to the wisdom of "not judging a book by its cover," as many non-Japanese have had to learn by trial and error from living and working among the Japanese.

Verbal communication, especially of concepts and ideas, is far less important in Japan than it is in the West, even among the well educated. Japanese live in a culture that fosters elegant, standardized human interchange and teaches people to project to others a formal persona using an established calculus of standardized words and gestures. Only in private and with people they feel comfortable with are the Japanese likely to reveal the many faces—gritty, funny, wacky, creative, sensuous, intuitive, easy-going, sharp, perceptive, kindly—of their real humanity.

3

READING
THE JAPANESE MIND:
Ways of Thinking
Beyond Logic

*The Japanese way of thinking is world's distant from ours.
They put sentiment before logic, believe the end often justi-
fies the means, and have a unique "coping" mode of problem analysis and solution that is alien to Western modes of
thinking. They can be both suggestible and gullible to a
marked degree, but highly original thinkers when working
in small spaces.*

Certainly the most common concern of Westerners who deal with
or have relationships with Japanese is how they think. Businesspeople, foreign academics, diplomats, officials, and even those
who work or live daily with the Japanese lament their lack of
understanding of the way they think. Ernesto Szasz, married to a
Japanese woman for fifteen years, said, "Once the honeymoon
period ended, I spent the next ten years trying to understand where
my wife was coming from. Part of the problem is that she, like so
many Japanese, refuses to communicate what she is thinking or
feeling, or, which is hardly any better, gives me *tatemae* explanations,

which explain nothing. It has been a very painful process for me, and for her too. I'm surprised that we are still together." Carlton Patrick, employed by a Japanese securities company in Tokyo and a longtime bilingual resident, confided, "I am still regularly surprised how I misjudge what my Japanese colleagues are thinking, or what their motivations are."

In his book *The Other Hundred Years War* (1983), Russell Braddon stated that defeat at the battle of Midway "was the fault of the Japanese temperament, the flaws in which produce chronic rivalries, unpredictable lapses of concentration, fatal delusions of invincibility and an incorrigible aversion to any departure from an agreed plan." Author Jared Taylor, who was born and raised in Japan, wrote, "Hazy Japanese thinking is supposed to be related to Japan's emphasis on nonverbal communication. In Japan ... it is very important to be able to dope out the feelings and sense the emotions of a situation.... Many Japanese distrust eloquence and pure logic" (1983).

The Japanese themselves are well aware that the "Japanese way of thinking" differs from that of Westerners. Takao Suzuki, a senior manager in the Toshiba group, told me that, "We Japanese have been brought up according to Buddhism and Confucianism for over a thousand years. But the basis of European ideas is Christianity. Since we know nothing about that religion and are not conscious of how they differ from us, there are many times when we do not understand their way of thinking." The writer, former parliamentarian, and commentator Masao Kunihiro (1980) reported that the Japanese have an "esthetics of silence" which makes "a virtue of reticence and a vulgarity of verbalization or open expression of one's inner thoughts."

SENTIMENT BEFORE RATIONALITY

If a phrase were to convey the most distinctive, typical quality of the Japanese way of thinking, it would be "sentiment (or feelings) before rationality." Sentiments run deep in Japan. The Japanese have strong sentiments and feelings for Japan the nation, the land itself (most Japanese living overseas want to be buried in Japan, for example), their hometown (*furusato*), their old schools, colleges, and classmates, their mothers, for themselves as honorable, sincere, hardworking individuals, and not least their companies, their clients, and the seniors to whom they have become attached. The key factor underlying sentiment is really an attachment bordering on possessiveness. Japanese culture is very much an attachment culture. It fosters a powerful, lifelong emotional grip on and identification with people and groups critical to personal well-being, social status, social identity, group and family membership, and conformity to the group. Psychiatrist Keigo Okonogi wrote in an article in *Japan Echo* (1978) that "a connection once formed [in Japan] between people cannot be easily severed...."

The long-running arguments between pro-whaling Japanese and those opposed to whaling are a good example of how the Japanese use sentiment. Whaling is obviously a very emotional issue for the Japanese, and their two most commonly used arguments are that Japanese culture is under threat and that the Japanese are being treated unfairly. The culture-threat argument runs like this: consumption of whales (and whaling itself) makes up an "age-old cultural tradition," and that without understanding that cultural background, other countries are set on destroying Japanese culture. Accusations of unfair treatment, put forward as legitimate reasons why Japan should be allowed to resume whaling, can be highly sentimental and melodramatic: the whaling ban represents a threat to Japan's chopstick culture because while whale (and fish) meat can be eaten easily with chopsticks, the foreign implements knives and forks must be used to eat other meat needed to secure protein requirements. In addition, if Christians can eat turkey at Christmas, why should the Japanese in Wakayama stop drinking the traditional whale soup at New Year? No one argues that the slaughter of turkeys should be stopped. If Japanese are called savages because they eat whale, why are Christians not called savages for eating turkey?

Such arguments illustrate the Japanese preference for sentiment before logical argument. The logic in Japanese terms is clear: only a heartless person would dare to destroy an ancient, beautiful culture. Anyone with a heart therefore should readily agree to the lifting of the ban on whaling, or to any other emotionally charged, "survival-threatening" issue. The connection with the *naniwabushi* method of emotional persuasion described in Chapter 8 is obvious.

Sentiment is seen at work in Japanese appeals to what I call the *kantō* (fighting) spirit. When company sales are ailing, many company presidents appeal to an older tradition of response to problems, based on somewhat mindless pseudo-samurai values of the spirit being able to split rocks and pierce stones. Presidents in such cases often say to their workers: "Become devils! Be wild animals! Go out and fight!" This illustrates a lack of analytical sense, or an absence of strategy based upon analysis. There is still a widespread sentimental belief that all problems fall before a massive show of energy and determination.

Japanese are convinced that logic has little place in discussion when something deeply cherished is threatened. When there is a sense of threat and strong emotionality, the Japanese disdain neat, logical structures as unfeeling, unfriendly, and cold. They opt for more conversational, flowing argument in which their assumptions and premises will be revealed in due course, but not in the orderly way Westerners may be used to. The Japanese are also weak in conceptual arguments and the use of analogy, not because they are intellectually inferior, but because they use them so infrequently. When Japanese or foreigners do try to use concepts, analogies, and systematic logic, they find that they merely antagonize Japanese listeners by portraying themselves as cold, unfeeling, and inhuman.

TIES OF BLOOD

Japaneseness is treasured by most Japanese, and in the case of "Japanese blood" this means that genetic inheritance is seen as the basis of culture and language. A common expression, *"Nihonjin no chi ga nagarete iru*" (the blood of Japanese is flowing on), implies that Japanese blood is the spiritual vehicle of Japanese culture. Mannari and Befu (1983) observed that "the racial purity of the Japanese is, as they see it, the result of genetic continuity through generations, stretching ... far back in history."

Is this rational? Can such views be scientifically sustained? Absolutely not. Once third-generation Japanese-Americans or Japanese-Brazilians, for example, visit or live in Japan, most finally accept that they are indeed Americans or Brazilians, and that any Japaneseness they thought they possessed in the United States or Brazil was only an illusion. Contrast this with the Japanese view that everyone with Japanese blood in their veins ought to be able to speak Japanese fluently. It is a great shock for Japanese in Japan to discover that people of Japanese ancestry from abroad cannot speak Japanese, and have personalities that do not mesh with Japanese culture. If these overseas Japanese stay on in Japan, they can face considerable difficulties. If they wish to teach English (or Portuguese or Spanish), they may be passed over in favor of Caucasians, based on reasoning that since they are Japanese, they could not speak their native language as well as a Caucasian. If they become managers in foreign companies in Japan, they are expected by their Japanese staff to side with them against the head office in any disputes that arise.

ROLE PLAYING AND THOUGHT PROCESSES

How the Japanese think cannot be understood until it is recognized that much of "official" or *tatemae* behavior in business or government is actually role playing and that their way of thinking is dictated by what is commonly accepted as the correct or proper way to play the role. It can be shown how pervasive this is by listing some of my own most common personal experiences or knowledge of Japanese role playing.

    1. Saying nice things to visitors, foreigners, and seniors. An example is saying to foreigners, "Nihongo ga ojōzu desu ne" *(your Japanese is fluent), when in fact it is pathetically inadequate.*

This is entirely role-playing behavior. The thought behind such behavior is to make people feel comfortable, valued, and at ease. In their early days in Japan, foreigners may really believe that they speak Japanese well and are personally attractive to the Japanese. Much later on they discover that the Japanese behavior had nothing to do with them personally but was only the playing of a standardized host or service role in Japanese society.

2. Japanese young people act demurely and respectfully at first or early meetings, but later it is discovered that their personalities and interests are vastly different.

In Japan, young people learn that those who are most "successful" socially are those who are pleasant, smiling, demure, flexible, and quick-witted. Those who behave like *iiko* (good children) probably learned at an early age to behave in ways that pleased parents and teachers. Among young women, there is also a variant of the "good child" role, called the *burikko*, or "mannered" child. *Burikko* girls are instantly recognizable to other Japanese: they are deliberately cute and doll-like and speak with an artificial, high-pitched cadence. The social behavior of *iiko buri* and *burikko* is perceived by other Japanese as superficial and artificial, stemming from a well-learned role.

3. Lionizing foreigners who know little or nothing about Japan, making exaggerated claims for Japan, and giving lavish gifts with the view that sometime in the future a return favor may be requested.

Obviously, foreigners are viewed with a different mindset by the Japanese. They believe that foreigners must be treated differently, as visitors, as people who do not understand Japan, or as people who might be useful as "pets" or objects to display to other Japanese. That the initial lionizing and flattery were only calculated role playing is discovered when some Japanese cut whatever emotional connection foreigners imagined had been established by using silence, avoidance, or manifest disinterest.

ROLE PLAYING AMONG THE JAPANESE

Although everyone plays roles in life, the Japanese are required to play more roles, more often, and more meticulously. There is a manifest high degree of acting in Japanese life in the contacts between people. A lot of this acting is rule following, fitting in, and adjusting to others. As mentioned in Chapter 2, Japan is a culture of reciprocal roles. In most situations, the Japanese expect themselves (have been conditioned) to behave according to accepted social norms and roles. To clarify why the Japanese spend so much more time role playing than do other nationalities, three types of roles and role playing can be discussed: 1) casual role playing, where roles are played in anonymous situations such as among passengers on a bus or in a queue, customers in a bank or shop, or spectators at a sports match; 2) ritual role playing, of standardized but simple roles such as waiter or shop assistant, with a low degree of inner involvement while maintaining external standardized behavior, gestures, etc.; and 3) involved role playing, with a high level of involvement in complex, demanding, and long-term roles, with the role player maintaining the performance throughout his/her contact with the other parties.

In Japan, wives play involved roles in relation to their husbands, especially if they have high social status. There is a hostess role, which includes standardized ways to greet guests, make guests feel at home, conduct light conversation, serve food or snacks, and see guests off. The level of involvement is demonstrated in the following story.

A company president kept a mistress in addition to his wife and grown family, and gradually the custom emerged of him spending three consecutive nights each week with the mistress. On the morning of the day he was to go to his mistress's apartment, his wife invariably packed his bag for him and saw him off as though he were going on a trip. After the mistress had a child, each week the wife would also include something—a toy or sweets or clothing—for the child.

Involved role playing is common where the status gap is great. Examples are secretaries to politicians, research assistants and junior academics to professors, pharmaceutical sales personnel to medical practitioners, sales people to major buyers, apprentices, assistants, chauffeurs, etc., to people of distinction (*erai hito*). Role playing must be invariably consistent on the subordinate side. To step out of an involved role means losing it permanently. This is much less likely with casual or ritual roles. The point of this discussion of roles is that in so many cases in Japan how an individual thinks is dictated not by his or her individualistic qualities, but by the nature of the role being played.

HOW JAPANESE ORGANIZE THEIR IDEAS

A major problem for the Japanese in organizing their ideas is that they grow up in a society where no one challenges them or expects them to think or question, to be logical or systematic. Education is simply retention of rote learning. At no time during their school or college days, or during their working life for that matter, are they challenged in the way Westerners are. Toshio Azuma, chairman of Tokyo International College, said of his own graduate education in the United States:

> I remember vividly how awful my university papers were, returned to me with comments like, "Unintelligible," "Why?" "Who says so?" I had no idea how to write a logical paper. No such discipline exists in the Japanese university system ... my thesis adviser ... made me rewrite what I thought was a finished product over twenty times! During

that ordeal, I was gradually weaned from indirectness and vagueness, things I had always thought proper.

This brought back memories for me. I have made comments like those Azuma mentioned countless times in grading Japanese essays and theses, irrespective of whether they were in English or Japanese. Reading over my comments again, and recalling the social environment of Japan, I felt a certain embarrassment because my values and background are so obviously distant from the Japanese as to make my detailed critiques seem almost insulting, but I believed that I had no choice other than to assess and criticize in the way of the Western scholarly tradition.

Yoshihiko Kobayashi is a famous French scholar in Japan. Sometimes he is called upon to take part in giving French *viva-voce* examinations of Japanese students seeking entry to French universities. He sits in on interviews by French professors or French cultural attaches, of which the following is typical:

"Will you go to France?"
"Yes, I will."
"What is your purpose?"
"When I was a freshman, I became interested in nineteenth-century French literature, so I entered the French literature school. As a graduate student I now specialize in the study of Balzac. Therefore, to deepen my knowledge of French language and literature, I wish to study at the University of Paris."

Each interview continues in this vein, and by the end of each the French examiner is obviously irritated. Asked why, the typical answer is, "They don't give straightforward answers to my questions." What the French would prefer is a conversation like the following:

"Will you go to France?"
"Yes, I will."
"Will you tell me your purpose?"
"To study French language and literature."

"Will you tell me about that in more detail?"
"Yes, I want to study nineteenth-century French novels,
especially Balzac."
"Where do you wish to study?"
"At the University of Paris."

The difference between the two dialogues, of course, is that the
French want the conclusion to come first, whereas the Japanese
want the context to be stated first, on the presumption that the conclusion cannot really be understood until the context is clear. But
to the French and other Westerners who do communicate in this
way, the Japanese way sounds circuitous, or even evasive. In the
Japanese-Western business organization context, conflicts like
this are commonplace, because each party uses contrasting but
thoroughly mastered and customary parts of their own culture.
A Japanese who answered questions from another Japanese in the
French manner would be regarded with as much suspicion as are
Japanese students by French examiners.

In a more general sense, the cultural difference demonstrates
the greater Japanese sensitivity to context, which means that they
are much more interested to learn about human motivations than
seems the case with the more linear Western style epitomized by
the original sample dialogue. When Westerners begin to work for
Japanese companies, they too learn that they must structure proposals in the Japanese way: first, the background or origin of the
idea or proposal, then how it has developed, how others have
become involved, the current status of thinking, and finally the
proposal itself, including recommendations, costs, conclusions, or
requests.

COPING: A PIECEMEAL STRATEGY FOR SURVIVAL

Japan is a coping society. Put another way, the Japanese believe
that the safest way to survive and prosper in their society, as well
as in the international order, is to make the "minimum adjustments

needed to neutralize or overcome criticism and adapt to the existing situation with the fewest risks" (Blaker, undated). This is given
more attractive labels by the Japanese, such as compromise, or give
and take, which demand an equal sharing of pains by both sides
(if pains there be) or equal concessions on both sides, or concessions
on the side that has less to lose. Michiko Nakahara, a Japanese psychologist friend who spent much time abroad, agrees, although she
expressed it differently:

> The Japanese in everyday life do not want to face problems
> or difficulties, so [they] try to get by with the minimum of
> change. The way they approach problems is something like
> tacking in yachting—you don't try to go directly into the
> wind, but progress slowly forward by going from side to
> side. Japanese culture makes people fearful of tackling any-
> thing head on in case someone is offended. So they fiddle
> with problems, approach them indirectly.

When challenged to open markets or increase quotas, for example, the Japanese have repeatedly offered the absolute minimum,
claiming it was the best they could offer. Anything more than the
minimum has been felt to be too risky, although eventually powerful opponents like the United States have forced the Japanese to
make repeated concessions and they have ended up looking insincere and untrustworthy.

James Fallow (1989) cited a typical example of the Japanese
coping approach. This occurred when British seats on the Tokyo
Stock Exchange were being negotiated, and was reported to
Fallows by a Briton involved in the negotiation.

> [The British] position was that, in principle, any company
> that met the financial and other standards should be allowed
> to enter the market. Each time we said that, the Japanese
> reply was, "How many seats do you want?" We would say,
> "We don't know how many, we want it to be open to any
> qualified applicant." And they would say, "Do you want two

seats? Do you want three?" The British negotiators eventually decided that two British companies seemed qualified, so
they told the Japanese, "We want two." The Japanese side
went back to deliberate—and in that time another qualified
British firm appeared. They came back to us and said that
two would be all right—but by this time we were asking for
three. They were incensed at us for not sticking to our word
and not knowing what we wanted. I'm sure they thought it
was a case of Western deception. The principle of free entry
never had a chance.

The Japanese preference for a coping, minimalist approach
seems obvious here. Unlike the reporter, I do not see their reaction
as suspicion of Western deception. The frontline Japanese would
have been under pressure from their seniors to keep foreign participation to a "minimum." A firm Japanese "position" or upper limit
that they were required to hold to satisfy the general risk-minimizing strategies that the Japanese conventionally display in all such
situations was unlikely. When that position, in this case two seats,
was threatened, the frontline Japanese faced possible rebuke,
criticism, and loss of face for not being able to stem or minimize
demands.

Japan specialist Michael Blaker has been a leader in helping to
explain Japanese diplomatic behavior. He has said that their behavior is based on a tendency to feel totally defenseless when faced by
powerful outsiders (an observation that fits exactly with the views
of psychiatrist Keigo Okonogi). Blaker (undated) reported that former Foreign Minister Saburo Okita devised the following strategy
in 1974: Japan must accept that it was defenseless on every side
(happō yabure) and therefore had to "avoid becoming a danger to
any country in the world." When the Japanese entered the Law of
the Sea Conference in 1977, they adopted a deliberately ambiguous, defensive posture toward the 200-mile economic zone concept
and entered the conference with no ideas or proposals concerning
the zone, indeed with nothing but an intention to play the "coping"

game, or to wait and see. When the vote was taken on the zone issue, Japan found itself the only one of 115 countries to vote against it. By that, it had truly become defenseless on all sides, and, having no ideas or proposals, was unable to work behind the scenes in committees to negotiate a settlement to its advantage.

This coping style continued to mark Japan's participation in subsequent Law of the Sea Conferences. For example, Japan's ambassador at the next meeting six months later told reporters on arriving in Geneva: "I have no particular instructions. I'll watch the situation and ask Tokyo what to do." The then Foreign Minister Kiichi Miyazawa also said publicly, "We'll go with the flow of the conference." In fact, Japan did have a secret agenda, namely to limit the extension of territorial waters to twelve miles, but negotiators were so wedded to their coping strategy that they made no attempts to persuade others to accept the twelve-mile limit. Thus their approach through this and subsequent conferences was cautious and disengaged from the behind-the-scenes negotiations. Eventually, in spite of being one of the great maritime powers, Japan found itself swept along and forced to accept the 200-mile zone.

In his analyses of Japan's performance at this and other international conferences, and in its participation as a contributor to the Gulf War, etc., Blaker has shown some of the costs of Japan's minimalist coping style. For one, its efforts are unappreciated: "Japan, whose driving motive is placating or accommodating others … ends up pleasing no one." In addition, the coping approach consumes so much time in collecting information and clarifying others' views and policies that the Japanese fall behind the progress of the conferences. At the same time, the tedium of its approach stirs distrust and resentment in others.

The minimalist coping strategy used in Japanese diplomacy stems directly from the mainstream culture, where compromise has always been valued over dispute or argument. Compromise in Japan is very much a sentiment-driven activity, since it is aimed at preserving good human relationships. The common expression "*gojo gojō*" (mutual cooperation and compromise) is lauded as a virtue to a much greater degree than "give and take" in the West. *Gojo gojō* means reaching decisions through a display of goodwill, by mutual trust, and reaching some final, mutually acceptable position by way of fine adjustments of one's position or demand. Coping is also connected to the notion of *kaizen*, or improvement (see Chapter 10). *Kaizen* implies continuous fine changes, rather than one categorical revision or sudden innovation. Masaaki Imai (1989) wrote that, "*Kaizen* signifies small improvements made in the status quo as a result of ongoing efforts." It is "a concept so natural and obvious to many Japanese managers that they often do not even realize that they possess it." In contrast, *kaizen* is "nonexistent or at the very least weak" in the West, otherwise how could Western factories "remain exactly the same for a quarter of a century?" Western companies believe, asserted Imai, in the "great leap forward approach," in other words, innovation and a great attention-getting process, whereas *kaizen* "is often undramatic and subtle … its results seldom immediately visible." The connection to coping will be obvious, as will the conclusion that both coping and *kaizen* can only be successful in a monocultural Japanese environment.

SUGGESTIBILITY AND GULLIBILITY BEFORE INDEPENDENT THOUGHT

To achieve a comprehensive understanding of how the Japanese think, different levels of their national personality must be examined. In discussing the suggestibility of the Japanese, the focus is not on issues but on overt submissiveness. Gregory Clark (1986) has written that Japanese are a "simple people, group oriented and situational, with little interest in logic and argued principles—due to the absence of ideological pressure on the society for much of its history." Part of the Japanese postwar economic and societal success (low crime rates, excellent mental health, etc.) has been due to this very suggestibility and gullibility, although as more worldly

Japanese grow older their suggestibility does become overlain with skepticism and suspicion of others.

Suggestibility implies readiness to do as one is told promptly without questioning. It is abetted by the command or vertical structure of the society and organizations, as well as by still-meaningful traditional values such as *messhi hōkō* (destroying the self and serving others). This suggestibility flows directly out of Japanese compliance behavior. It makes them easy to direct, organize, and mobilize in the pursuit of major goals. The dependency they learn as they grow up, especially dependence upon people they have obligations to, is not unreasonably viewed as akin to "brainwashing," and there is enough use of the term brainwashing (*sennō*) among Japanese to indicate a genuine sense of personal susceptibility to being artfully persuaded or intimidated by others.

The shared, stereotyped views about "what sort of people we are" that are held by many Japanese are a good example of gullibility at work. For example, qualities of character like diligence, tidiness, and politeness are regarded as ingrained or "in the blood," rather than as culturally acquired or learned. Japanese are group oriented whereas Westerners are individualists, and all individualists are egotists; Westerners are born to accept that confrontation is natural; Japanese love and respect form. These are all popular stereotypes. But when I have asked for examples, children or sports figures have been pointed out as illustrating the Japanese "natural" love of form by wearing uniforms or conforming to instructions. That the Japanese themselves rarely appreciate that much of this so-called Japanese behavior stems from rules, the violation of which brings punishment, is rather beside the point being made here: that most of the self-stereotypes of the Japanese reflect their gullibility or their readiness to accept a popular opinion and viewpoint without independent judgment.

While growing up as a Japanese does not encourage independent critical thought, it does encourage being in touch with popular opinion and with what is in fashion in ideas, behavior, and appearance. When the capacity for critical independent thought is poorly developed, human beings are susceptible to scams, superstitions, and brainwashing, and few, it seems, more so than the Japanese.

In the past decade in Japan major scams have been uncovered in door-to-door selling at inflated prices of personal seals, and pots, gold temples, and bejewelled pagodas for use on family altars, as well as the growth industry of temples set up solely to sell religious services for aborted fetuses to guilt-ridden women, in a land where more than one million women have abortions annually. Professor Sadao Asami (1989), an authority on one of those scams under-taken by the Unification Church in the 1980s, has called the Japan-ese people "the most gullible in the world." Data he provided me, showing that the Japanese were ten to twenty times more likely (on a population pro rata basis) to be deceived by door-to-door sales-people than other nationalities, support his view.

"UNNATURAL" THINKING AND THE JAPANESE

A social or educational system that produces a society of con-formists, camp followers, yes-men, or "suckers" must also applaud conformist ideologies and thinking. But while the behavior of Japanese is conformist, their ideas are not. Overt behavior is trained and etiquette and manners are prescribed, but individuals are left free, as Finkelstein (1991) pointed out, "to follow a leader with whom he or she deeply agrees," or to imagine whatever they want to. Although taboo behavior is taboo behavior wherever it occurs, the Japanese seem to have an unusual freedom to imagine in private whatever they want to, and this helps them to be able to "think the unthinkable," even about taboos.

The case of Issei Sagawa, the self-confessed cannibal who killed and feasted upon the body of his German teacher in Paris in 1981, is especially illustrative. While most Japanese say they regard Sagawa as a "devil," "monster," or "freak," there is a coterie of writers and intellectuals today that sympathizes with him as someone who has transcended civilized borders and defied taboos.

Arrested in Paris for the crime he openly confessed to, Sagawa was declared legally insane in France in 1983, and all criminal charges were dropped. A year later, the French declared him an untreatable psychotic and repatriated him to Japan. After two years in a Japanese hospital, he was freed in 1985 and has been free ever since. The Japanese police claim that they are unable to charge him with any crime because the French will not hand over the dossier of evidence. Now Sagawa lives as a writer and was even issued a passport in 1992 to visit Germany, where he became a star guest on a television show. One of his supporters, psychologist Shu Kishida, takes the view that:

> Eating human flesh is the same thing as assimilating your-self to the body you are eating. In the Western world there are many historical cases in tribes that you eat the flesh of the man you respect. In Sagawa's case *it is a extreme form of the inherent admiration of every Japanese for the white race* (McGill, 1992; italics added).

In an interview with the English journalist Peter McGill (1992), Sagawa observed:

> For Japanese girls, I haven't any sexual desire. I am feeling as if she is my own daughter, no, sister, so it would be inces-tuous. For Occidentals though, I have a big admiration. The style, physically, I find very sexual ... I don't think that's so exceptional; almost all Japanese have a complex towards Western people ... I prefer big women, but they are also repulsive.

What Sagawa demonstrates is an extreme capacity to "think the unthinkable" in the privacy of his own mind, although he has inter-estingly balked at incest. Although he is called a monster by some Japanese, his 1983 book about his crime sold 200,000 copies in Japan. A book by the playwright Juro Kara, entitled *Letters from Sagawa*, and based on his correspondence with Sagawa while he was still in hospital in Paris, won Japan's most prestigious literary award, selling 320,000 copies in the first month. Whatever is said, there is no doubting the fascination and even awe that Japanese have toward Sagawa.

One important element of this fascination stems from the lack of taboos or even revulsion in Japan toward the consumption of raw fish. Sagawa wrote in his book of how he had talked to his victim about "my love of raw meat." After killing her he wrote (McGill, 1992):

> I wondered where I should eat first. I ate right in the center of the abundant, bouncing part of the right hip ... but I could not bite it out.... So I picked up a fruit knife from the kitchen.... Finally I was eating beautiful white woman, and thought nothing was so delicious. Then I moved to the other thighs.

For all the horror of the situation, other Japanese are able to identify with tasting a new variety of raw flesh. Eating raw fish, whale, horse, beef, and sometimes rare meats like bear and snake is a familiar part of Japanese food consumption culture. Curiosity about the taste of meats unknown or rare in Japan, such as crocodile, dog, monkey, kangaroo, or goat, is common. In northern Hokkaido, there is a little timber inn on the banks of the Ransu River called the Takasago Restaurant. Its specialty is sea lion, eaten raw or grilled. In season Hokkaido brown bear and two kinds of seal are on the menu. Members of the imperial family are said to be listed as Takasago customers.

So it is no surprise that some Japanese should express amused curiosity about the taste of human flesh, especially if relaxed and a little tipsy. After all, the connection between foods, particularly raw ones, and sexual behavior or genitals is not unknown to the Japanese. Added to this is the extreme taste sensitivity of the Japanese, who believe that "to find and enjoy a new flavor adds seventy-five days to your life." But there is no more compulsion to sample human flesh among them than there is anywhere else. In brief, then, what may seem an "unnatural" way of thinking to Westerners links into aspects of Japanese mainstream culture that are highly compelling and sensuous for many Japanese, although they can also create a platform for obsessive, darker behavior.

EMERGING NEW WAYS OF THINKING

Within the mainstream society of young, well-educated Japanese, significant, irreversible changes are emerging in ways of thinking. In some respects, these changes have been made easier by the typical Japanese capacity to think what they like. Experiencing less social pressure from their parents and peers than earlier generations, the young generation is changing its way of thinking, as detected in research undertaken by the advertising agency Hakuhodo. One of their reports (cited in Masao Maruyama, 1985) describes the main orientation of young Japanese as the "switchboard" approach to life, in which the individual becomes the designer of his or her own lifestyle. Below are six strategies or ways of thinking identified by Hakuhodo.

Summit Strategies

Summit strategists are concerned with being the best that one can be (that is, by reaching a summit) in the physical, economic, cultural, intellectual, or sensory fields. Physical summits can be achieved by plastic surgery, body building, wearing a wig, or even getting a perfect suntan. Cultural summits include becoming an expert in some esoteric field of knowledge, such as the occult, ancient myths, or computer science.

Manic Strategies

Manic strategies are employed to counter identity diffusion or confusion. They include "doing something seriously because it is fun," or discovering fun in something outdated, conventional, or unexpected, such as farming, taking slow trains instead of express trains, or owning no possessions.

Scanning Strategies

The wish for metamorphosis, such as becoming a film star, hero, or unusual personality, avoiding deep involvement in any relationship, or hiding one's true skills only to give a surprise performance and command instant respect from others at a later time are elements of scanning strategies. The metamorphosis wish is related to long-standing Japanese fascination with supernormal powers, while the pretense of lacking skill is a perverse reaction to traditional modesty and lack of ostentation.

Handling Strategies

Handling strategies include taking initiative, acting in anticipation of something, taking care of, and fixing up, but exclude any connotation of manipulating other people. The purpose of these strategies is to develop automatic response patterns for all social situations, such as dating, sex, and interactions with parents and seniors, so that no intellectual or emotional involvement is needed.

Restatement Strategies

Restatement strategies can be both positive and negative. Positive ones include: revivalism; finding new applications for traditional systems and methods; endurance; carrying out tasks however difficult or impossible they may appear; outspokenness, which includes deliberate exhibitionism in perverse contravention of traditional mores; and nostalgia or the cultivation of retrogressive values and objects, such as music, books, or decorations. Negative strategies include: argument deflection and question begging, common among teenagers still at school; and bribery to correct social problems, which may include monetary gifts as well as favors.

Safe-niche Strategies

Softening of personal tastes and values and a generally spineless approach to life are typical of safe-niche strategies. Safe-niche people may be disappointed in their own abilities, and these strategies appear to free them from anxiety and permit emotional detachment.

These ways of thinking reflect many traditional Japanese personality traits, brought to center stage as it were by the crumbling or absence of central values in contemporary Japan. Single-minded absorption, avoidance and retreat, and various perverse reactions to central values are alternatives. There is increasing interest in the concepts of "breeding" and "incubation." Commenting on this, Maruyama (1985) wrote that:

> Indoor horticulture, in which plants are treated as family members, has become popular for breeding ... a subconcept of breeding is do-it-yourself activities incorporating one's own design in, for example, interior decoration. Thus breeding includes discovery, sponsorship, and design.

These tendencies taken in conjunction point to a developing destandardization of Japanese life.

In group-oriented behavior, Hakuhodo reports suggested that peer group members are increasingly only-children who strive to be recognized by others in the group for the special skills they can each contribute. This means that there is no absolute pecking order in the group and that the group exercises less peer group pressure on individual behavior, so that there is no hard and fast conformity pressure. This is not to say that the Japanese peer group is disntegrating. Rather, it is being adapted to the special needs of increasing individuality in Japanese ways of thinking among well-educated young people.

COMMENTS

To understand the thinking of the Japanese, one must first understand "where they are coming from." Easiest to misunderstand is that much Japanese thinking stems not from economic, logical, or rational considerations, but from sentiments about and attachments to people, groups, ideals, and connections valued for themselves. When sentiment is involved, the Japanese will readily consider that the end (such as the protection of something treasured) can justify the means. This is frequently seen in their use of situational ethics. If, for example, a Japanese company employee is ordered by a superior to offer an (illegal) payment to secure, say, the movement of goods from a wharf in a third country, or to secure an order from competitors, there will be no hesitation in following orders. Faced with the decision without a superior being present, a Japanese will typically make the payment, justifying it, as many have done to me, by saying,

> I do it for the company's sake, not my own. I have no right to let my personal ethics interfere with the more important task of ensuring the continuity of the company. Failure to secure that order could be the difference between the collapse or survival of my company.

How the Japanese think in a particular situation can often be understood by determining the social or occupational role being played at the time. In some roles, most of what is said is *tatemae* and not meant to be taken at face value, although at times it may be an expression of positive sentiment and even esteem. At other times, the real meanings will be understood by those with the experience to "break the code."

Looking at "thinking" as a form of information search and decision making, it is important for foreigners to be aware of how often the "coping" mode of problem analysis and solution is used by the Japanese. Questions are one aspect of coping. Those which non-Japanese might be asked in their home countries and take to signify special interest in the individual or their wares on the part of the questioner in Japan are often no more than questions that have been asked a dozen times before of others. Coping that involves making minimum adjustments (what the Japanese call *kodashi ni suru*), is a culturally typical approach to problem solving that foreigners, whatever their connection to the Japanese, need to understand. Not to do so from the beginning is to tread a virtually certain path to confusion and ultimate resentment.

If businessmen from larger companies are excluded, it is true to say that the Japanese are a particularly suggestible, gullible people. Living the sheltered life that they do in their society, this is not surprising. Relaxing with them, I and other foreigners will at times say outrageously outlandish things to Japanese, to find many taking us seriously. At times, when asked where my ancestors came from, I have said things like, "Well, my great grandmother was a kangaroo (or koala)," and the response has often been a serious, bemused look (especially at my ears). Very few Japanese have ever expressed skepticism or laughed scornfully.

Finally, in examining "unnatural" thinking, taboos, and the emerging ways of thinking of young Japanese, those parts of the Japanese psyche that are free, private, and creatively fertile are exposed. Call it what we will, the capacity to "think the unthinkable," to think laterally, and to explore the cognitive aspects of novel paradigms offer a glimpse into the national genius of the Japanese.

4

PADDLING DUCKS AND TRANQUIL DUCKS: Elegance and Self-Expression in Japan

The Japanese pokerface is a modern phenomenon. It stems from the samurai tradition and, more recently, the insistence on standardization and precision. Underneath, however, the Japanese can be as expressive and joyous as others. This chapter helps to show this more human face of the Japanese.

To what should we attribute the elegance and sophistication of much of Japanese civilization and social etiquette? They stem greatly from two underappreciated facts: first, the Japanese are meticulously taught from childhood to regard the expression of uncensored, crude emotion and tactless comments that might offend others as uncivilized; and second, they are drilled in replacing uncensored emotions or tactless words with an often elegant repertoire of manner, etiquette, and formalized expressions.

Those of us reared in societies where the direct expression of emotion is respected as healthy and is eulogized as honest may find Japan in this respect an alien culture. In Japan, boys are taught that a man is only permitted tears on two occasions in his life: on the death of his parents, and on the death of his children. As a man working for a company, he will be expected to adopt a dry business-is-business attitude throughout the day. Meetings will not be characterized by jokes or attempts at light relief, which would be regarded as irresponsible. In the appraisal of projects, it is cold-eyed analysis, not enthusiasm, that is expected.

Girls are given more latitude, as elsewhere. But a Japanese mother is still expected to set a stoic model for her children. Although women reject outright those feudal days when a bride had to live submissively under the grim eye of her mother-in-law, the culture continues to hold up the ancient motherly role model of self-sacrifice and rocklike fortitude. Values like these underlie the words of a popular song about wartime pilots ready to sacrifice themselves for their country:

> You are the suicide pilot's mother
> So please don't cry
> Laugh as you send us off
> We'll show you how to die
> Mother, oh Mother!

The cultural heritage of Japan is replete, even in today's peacetime society, with examples of self-denial, of mothers putting on brave faces, or of those modern warriors (now rapidly disappearing), the salarymen who sacrifice their private lives for the company.

SUPPRESSION OF GRIEF

A few years ago, the infant son of an American friend in Japan died. His Japanese wife seemed almost jovial. Grieving deeply himself, he remonstrated angrily with her for failing to show grief over the infant's death. The wife dutifully responded by trying to contort her face into a mask of grief and shed tears, but he said that the result was more comical than sad. It was then that he understood that she, like so many people trained in self-suppression, had not developed her capacity to express personal grief. The general restraints on expressiveness in Japan can deny some people the chance to get in touch with their emotions.

The extremity of such restraint is seen in Noh drama, where deep grief or weeping is reduced to highly stylized actions: one hand held stiff and flat is slowly raised to within inches of the eyes, and then slowly lowered to signify wrenching grief. Noh drama is eons away from everyday life's pangs, but it illustrates how the Japanese can replace raw emotions with an elegant language of expression. Noh drama is contrived to purify human behavior: the face becomes a mask of indeterminate expression; voices are squeezed and dehumanized; and human movement is reconstructed into the sublime. Arts like Noh, flower arrangement, tea ceremony, and so on are the forms that the instinct to employ *tatemae* and put a good face on things take in elite Japanese culture.

This is not to say that grief, sadness, and tears are unfamiliar to or unexpressed by the Japanese; they are the most commonly expressed of all strong emotions. Anger and physical or verbal aggression, passionate excitement, or unbridled laughter are no-nos, but tears flow freely in Japan, especially in moments of high melo-drama. When a team or individual has fought valiantly but failed to win a coveted prize, when shame overwhelms the individual, or when people long separated are finally reunited, tears are shed without inhibition. Japanese grief is especially connected to rela-tionships of close, even cloying, attachment. The modern word for grief or sadness in Japan, *kanashii*, conveys a sense of deep attach-ment. In ancient times it meant a particularly tender, fulsome love for one's lover or children (*itoshiku omou kimochi*), with a conno-tation of being involuntary or beyond direct control. No other mode of Japanese emotional expression matches grief or sadness for forthrightness.

From a conventional modern Japanese viewpoint, the suppres-sion of grief by a mother who has just lost her child constitutes a positive contribution to the Japanese social order by allowing life to go on and not triggering any disabling or needless grief in others. But a cross-cultural setting complicates perceptions of behavior.

BARRIERS TO SELF-EXPRESSION

Japanese self-suppression causes uncertainty and concern in relationships with non-Japanese. For example, my Taiwanese tailor once told me: "We were taught in school that the Japanese are like ducks. They are calm on the water, but are paddling madly underneath." Englishman Gordon Hathaway, who deals daily with the Japanese in Tokyo as a metal broker says, "Dealing with the Japanese is like mental fencing. I cannot read their faces at all."

Although the Japanese pokerface is sometimes perceived by foreigners as a mask hiding their intentions, Japanese businessmen are aware of it as cultural behavior that they have little control of. They know that it creates problems in their dealings with non-Japanese, even when they have the best of intentions. Many try to be more expressive, but having been raised in a society that puts no value on facial expressiveness, those attempts often resemble those of my American friend's wife, looking comical or odd.

The pokerface is closely connected to Japanese attitudes to communication, as discussed in Chapter 2. One aspect of this, the problems that many people experience in becoming sociable and socially articulate, has universal significance. Shyness and the inability to speak up in public are acute problems among the Japanese. Japanese society positively discourages eloquence and articulateness, while warnings abound about the fate of people who are smooth talkers.

Among friends or with co-workers, most Japanese are able to relax, especially if alcohol is consumed. Company excursions to provincial tourist resorts offer opportunities to let the hair down. But when there is little intimacy, the brakes are usually well applied to social spontaneity; often a Japanese "party" is a very muted affair of stop-and-go conversation, nervous laughter, and awkward silences. Being the sophisticated, pragmatic society that it is, Japan provides cultural solutions to such occasions. When parties or celebrations are planned by companies, someone will be assigned to be the *taiko mochi* (professional jester), responsible for keeping the party going, organizing games, jollying the shy into participation, bridging events with amusing patter, and cheering the audience up. The *taiko mochi* can be hired for the occasion, although frequently one of the staff will play the role, and probably be very good at it. A number of books giving details of party games and valuable ideas for patter are available.

It was the recognition of problems in self-expression by a Japanese company president that led him to approach me some years ago to train twelve of its sales engineers. I was to help them develop the skills to survive in foreign lands and to communicate and negotiate effectively with foreign clients. The biggest barrier that had to be worked on was, the president said, their lack of personal expressiveness, the inability to be forthright or articulate about what they were thinking or feeling. When the course began, my trainees were indeed rather wooden and unexpressive as communicators in English, awkward and uneasy when speaking in public, far from spontaneous or rhythmical in their bodily movements, and bland and neutral in their facial expressions. By the end of the course, real changes and improvements were noted by everyone involved. How had this been achieved, and what did we learn from our three months together?

One of the most important activities was regular encounters with foreigners, in addition to myself. I insisted that each trainee go into the city regularly, meet and interview foreigners on the street, and then report back, telling us in detail what had happened and how the foreigners had reacted. This allowed them to recognize their stiffness and lack of spontaneity. In the classroom, we regularly worked on skills in observing and correctly interpreting the nonverbal behavior, especially facial expressions, of others. This helped them to recognize how well they had learned to suppress the expression of emotion. Individuals were asked to recall personal memories and emotions that were highly charged for them, and their partner in the exercise would be asked to observe from changes in their facial expression, usually about the eyes or mouth, whether the memories were positive or negative.

The results were eye-opening for the Japanese trainees as well as the Western instructor. Half of the trainees registered no discernible facial changes, even when they were recalling memories that they rated as painful or emotionally powerful. This suggested what I had only vaguely suspected before: that many Japanese are chronically expressionless or expression-incapable. The proportion was far higher than anything I had encountered in training Westerners and demonstrated that what is referred to as Japanese inscrutability is as much a concern for other Japanese as it is for foreigners who deal with them.

In the training program, I also used physical exercises regularly, especially disco dancing, to warm up or reenergize the trainees in after-lunch sessions. In the early stages of the course, many were manifestly only going through the motions of these unmasculine, unbusiness-like activities. One day I invited three young female dancers from an Indian-affiliated religious community in Japan to demonstrate to the trainees how they danced. As I had hoped, the dancers electrified the trainees. Their movements involved rapid, rhythmic, flowing arm and leg movements and sinuous hip movements, not to mention radiant facial expressions, as they created large arcs of movement throughout the room. It was in marked contrast to Japanese classical or folk dancing, which is sedate, earth-hugging, rhythmically simple, and highly economical of space. Soon, all the trainees were also dancing, as expressively as they could, and nobody was simply going through the motions. The personnel director, who had coincidentally just looked in, was similarly captivated and joined in as well. In fact, he danced more sinuously than anyone.

Given dynamic rhythms, colorful and sensuous females, and social approval of overtly expressive behavior, the Japanese prove to be as expressive as anyone else. But in the real world of Japan, social mores are against expressiveness. Anything that is flashy, gaudy, affected, smug, or conceited is frowned upon. By the values of Western societies, Japanese notions of what is flashy are constrained and conservative. For example, a Japanese who made a public speech that was characterized by good humor and energy would be labeled by many as *kiza*, which bears a range of pejorative meanings. Speaking in English with foreigners in an extroverted or enthusiastic way would be judged as *kiza* by other Japanese. A Westerner can wear a bright red necktie without comment, but it would be *kiza*, and a serious lapse of good taste, for a Japanese to do so. Avoiding *kiza* behavior is part and parcel of the general prohibitions against expressive or self-assertive behavior in Japan. Speaking up, or adopting a positive or enthusiastic stance or tone, is rarely encountered in Japan. Only *yakuza* (gangsters), professional sportsmen, or gamblers can get away with *kiza* behavior or dress.

PRECISION BEFORE EXPRESSION

In passing, it is fair also to say that the modern "gentrification" and constriction of Japanese society have also made people more precise and attentive to finer details, which have been important factors in the postwar successes of Japanese zero-defect mass manufacturing. The Japanese body in movement is disciplined. Like a machine tool, it is well controlled and precise, although it is also constrained, lacking in sinuosity and expressiveness. The Japanese have learned to use the extremities with precision and speed, but the rest of the body is passive. The upper torso plays little role in expression among the Japanese. When they dance, the movement is mainly in the hands and legs, not the hips, and no lateral movement of the body occurs.

Take the disciplined bodies of the modern Japanese, add to them the uniforms of the modern workplace, and the result is an array of human beings who look neat, take up little space, are quick to fit in, and do not create trouble. The disciplined Japanese workers of today are important statements about the modern mass-production/consumer culture. Standardized, neatly packaged, compact, and nonreactive, they are analogues of the superlative products they make in their factories. It is not surprising that they could be seen as "tranquil ducks." The typical blandness and lack of spontaneity that can create reliable mass-produced products also create human beings who can fit in well. But in this lies the real problem facing the Japanese, especially businessmen: They often seem colorless to non-Japanese. Their lack of expression also suggests to many non-Japanese that they lack friendly intent.

From my personal experience of the Japanese, I have learned that, in spite of surface appearances, underneath the Japanese are almost always good natured and well intentioned. Behind the pokerface one mostly finds simple passivity rather than any active calculation or intention to deceive.

Curiously, the unexpressive behavior of the Japanese has come in for public criticism in Japan when its oddity is revealed by international comparison. At both the 1984 and the 1988 Olympics the Japanese press was scathingly critical of the inhibited, spiritless movement of the Japanese contingent in the opening ceremonies, in contrast to the vigor and good humor of contingents from other countries. The Japanese press described their athletes at different times as "wooden soldiers," "neurotic," "uneasy," and "tense and unrelaxed." While coaches and coaching methods were blamed by the press, the fundamental problem lay in the inhibiting mores of the society itself. The Japanese press especially made a point of the fact that some non-Japanese athletes trained while listening to music on their Walkman personal stereos, although in conventional Japanese values such behavior would appear frivolous and insincere, and certainly would be forbidden by most Japanese coaches.

THE LESS-INHIBITED PAST

But the Japanese have not always been so inhibited. The late Ella Wiswell, an American anthropologist, was a student of Japan for forty-five years and lived there while doing research in 1935, 1951, and 1968 (Smith and Wiswell, 1982). She found that the gaiety and lively dancing among the country women she studied did not change between 1935 and 1951, but when she returned in 1968, they had become decorous and formal. Social control and the homogenization of the nation through mass education and mass media had extended into every corner of the nation by the postwar "economic miracle" era. This control included concepts of what a Japanese is, how a good Japanese should or should not behave, and the social conditioning that has created a well-organized, well-educated nation.

Until now, this kind of control has made postwar Japan a far cry from the prewar, premilitaristic society which had survived outside of Tokyo and its elitist samurai values for two thousand years or more. The Japan of yesterday was vigorous, uninhibited, expressive, and good natured, if often shameless by Western standards. Throughout the postwar period, the old Japan has withered but has not disappeared completely. Ecstatic dancing continues in some of the newer religions. Shamans who dance themselves into a deep trance to visit the world beyond are still found in remote parts of the country. Community dances at *Bon* festivals in July and August continue, and occasionally in remote areas retain some of the wild abandon of the premodern era.

The ancient practice of *hanami* (springtime cherry-blossom viewing) continues to be a national occasion for self-expression, dancing, singing, and good fellowship. *Hanami* brings out the latent good nature, playfulness, and innocence of the Japanese, and those who want to discover the enduring strengths of their folk culture should participate. *Hanami* not only survives, but the new folk pastime of *karaoke* has emerged to join it. Now enjoying a worldwide boom, *karaoke* is constantly evolving in Japan as an expressive medium for the people. *Karaoke* started in Japanese bars, but today the connection with alcohol has been broken. With the increasing variety of *karaoke*-related activities, such as clubs, teachers, practice rooms for rent, etc., the Japanese have developed a highly sophisticated new mode of personal expression to fit in with their traditional folk culture.

Ella Wiswell would be pleased with what is happening in Japan today. In 1968, she thought that the old Japan had been virtually snuffed out of existence. She regretted, as many did, what now appears to be only a temporary triumph by "elite" (samurai and Confucian) culture over folk culture, of centralized social control reinforced by notions of what is "good" behavior. For example, the Japanese team at the 1992 Winter Olympics was applauded by the Japanese press for its outgoing, relaxed, friendly manner (team members sprayed champagne wildly at medal ceremonies, among other things), in contrast to past Olympic teams. This was of profound importance to Japan, because that winter team set a precedent for international public behavior by the Japanese. Such precedents are critical to behavior change in Japan.

Outside the elite-oriented establishment, however, many Japanese today are free, creative, and expressive. Moreover, contemporary affluence, education, the bursting of the economic bubble, and new diversity in society are bringing Japan toward the end of its homogeneous, "reliable human product" stage. It is beginning to return to its folk culture roots, to greater personal expressiveness and directness, and non-Japanese will be allowed more often to see the true expressive face of the people.

5

BODY EFFICIENT: The Japanese Culture of Movement

How the Japanese walk, sit, use their hands, move, or remain still are clear-cut signs of what makes Japanese culture distinctive. Read their body language and one reads their hearts, minds, and values.

Living among the Japanese, one soon discovers that they are not only culturally different, but also subtly but clearly different in the way they move and use their hands, feet, head, and body. What human beings do with their bodies is as much a part of their culture as the way they show respect to others. The speed and dexterity of Japanese hands in handling everyday things or doing manual or craft work for which they have been trained are marked. Employees who giftwrap purchases in department stores amaze foreign tourists with their precise holding of the line of each fold of the paper and the strength and control exhibited in wrapping even large, heavy objects. Kindergarten children of four or five being taught to use scissors to cut paper or knives to sharpen pencils generally appear as clumsy as any other children. But in another year or two, it is hard not to be impressed by a class of Japanese first-graders cutting paper or sharpening pencils. By the time they have arrived in junior high school, most children have acquired the manual dexterity to wrap and tie up neatly any kind of parcel.

Manual skills are universally practiced in Japan. Those without basic skills are few, and lacking neatness and precision is a matter of shame. In Japan hands are implements rather than media of expression. As in English, the word hand (*te*) is used to symbolize skills (as in the English word "handy"), cooperation ("handshake"), manipulation ("handle"), pride in managing (as in "hands-on"), caring for things (also "handle"). In everyday Japanese culture for its tool functions, however, the hand is still central. In the traditional New Year game of *iroha karuta* (poem cards), an announcer reads out a proverb and the players' objective is to be the first to identify from among the cards spread out in front of them the one with the first syllable of the proverb, and flick it out of the area. In this game, quickness of observation, reflex speed, precision, and dexterity are everything if, as is usually the case, the players know what they are looking for. In a somewhat similar but more ancient game, called *hyakunin isshu* (single poems by one hundred poets), there are annual national competitions where the hand speed of competitors is dazzling.

Such elegant games, not to mention children's games like jacks using bones or stones, string games, finger flexing, and hand speed games, make manual dexterity of real importance in Japanese culture. Even in seemingly noncompetitive situations, dexterous hand movements serve useful ends. In jobs or crafts where tools are used, the tool becomes an object to wield cleverly in its own right. Railway clerks at ticket gates in Japan wield their ticket punches with speed and dexterity. When crowds pour through, the punch never stops clicking, since the clerk has built up a momentum. The clicking of the punch serves as a time killer when the number of passengers falls. With the introduction of automatic ticket gates, however, this is now a dying "art." Other workpeople or artisans, using knives, food choppers, chopsticks, fans, or hammers, also acquire and practice rhythms.

Once while visiting friends in Sapporo during a party, I offered to prepare deep-fried wonton, since Chinese cooking is a hobby of mine. My host accepted, and off I went to the kitchen, where I found all the ingredients I needed. I was involved in chopping spring onions and mincing pork on a wooden cutting board when the host and two or three guests suddenly burst into the kitchen, with rather unbelieving looks on their faces. "What was that noise?" one asked. "Who was doing that chopping?" With a very puzzled look on my face, I said, "I was." The host then said, "Oh, would you just keep doing it?" So I continued for a few moments as the three Japanese watched me. Then they broke into applause, and the host explained, "We have always thought that Westerners are very clumsy with their hands. When we heard the sound of chopping, we couldn't believe it, and had to come and see for ourselves."

This makes the point of how cultural the skillful use of implements is to the Japanese. For less worldly Japanese, the sight of a Westerner using chopsticks comfortably is also a great surprise. I confess to periodic irritation when told by surprised Japanese (or Chinese) that they are amazed at how well I use chopsticks, sometimes replying that I too was amazed that they could use knives and forks. That sort of remark tends to dampen conversation for a moment or two.

THE JAPANESE BODY

What the Japanese do with their bodies reflects what they do with their minds and souls. As long as the Japanese live in a society where self-control, restraint, and often self-sacrifice are demanded, they will impose such restraints and controls on their bodies.

But how do they do it? One of my earliest clues came from reading a 1970 book by cultural anthropologist Yuji Aida. He described an intriguing difference in total body behavior between Japanese and Westerners. When faced by some imminent threat, he noted, Westerners are prone to face the threat defiantly, and move their body weight forward. In contrast, the Japanese settle down into their lower body, turn their backs on the threat, squat in a tight ball, or put their arms over their heads, following the cultural avoidance precept of Japanese culture that "if you can't see it, it doesn't exist." Suppose, for instance, that you are in a very narrow, one-way street, and suddenly a car enters and comes rapidly toward you. You have nowhere to escape and the clearance on either side of the street is minute. According to Aida, if you are a Westerner you will probably face the car and stand defiantly. If you are a man and have women or children with you, you will put them behind you. On the other hand, if you are Japanese, you will turn your back to the car, try to incorporate children, etc., into your body form, then squat and roll your body up as much as possible into a ball.

This reversing/avoidance response, I have since learned, occurs throughout Japan. Some years ago, in a Japanese movie called *Eei ja nai ka?* about an actual incident of mass hysteria in the nineteenth century, a hysterical crowd was faced by troops with loaded rifles who seemed intent on killing them. The director did not have the crowd of several hundred run, scatter, or counterattack. He had them all behave like real Japanese: they turned their backs, squatted, and rolled themselves up into balls! In real life, in reaction to earthquakes or lightning at home, or to attackers in the street, the same thing occurs, unless there is space under a bed or in a cupboard in which to hide and experience a doubled feeling of security.

To understand the Japanese culture of bodily movement, it is necessary to recognize that Japanese and Western posture and movement are fundamentally different. Japanese posture is maintained by balance and control coming almost entirely from the buttocks and upper thigh muscles, with the weight distributed down through the leg and balanced on the foot just forward of the heel. Balance is much more important to the Japanese than to Westerners, and it is maintained by the split between the upper and lower halves of the body. In both sumo and judo, where the aim is to knock one's opponent off balance, enormous effort is made to develop a low center of gravity. When this is achieved, then the upper half of the body, especially the arms and shoulders, is free to grapple. Another way of thinking about the role of the lower half of the body is to see it as predominantly the buttocks and upper thigh area, or *koshi* in Japanese. The Chinese character for *koshi* has two parts, one meaning muscle, the other meaning linchpin or pivot. This indicates that the Chinese and Japanese have had a very good understanding of the bodily dynamics of balance since ancient times. Moreover, the word *koshi* has diverse implications in Japanese. If someone's buttocks are "low," he or she is modest and unassuming; if "high," lacking stability or firmness. If the buttocks are "light," someone is a quick starter; if "heavy," a slowcoach, a dillydallier. If someone is petrified by something, he or she can be said to have lost buttocks, meaning loss of balance, although more a common expression for the same thing is "the shoulders stiffen/harden."

This Japanese cultural way of achieving bodily balance also makes them prone to flatfootedness, by putting more stress on the foot behind the ball of the foot and so on the arch, but equally flatfootedness promotes physical stability. Westerners, in contrast, tend to find the point of balance closer to the ball of the foot. Internationally renowned stage director Tadashi Suzuki employs methods of acting training that illustrate this well. In 1992, under the auspices of the Japan Foundation, Suzuki took a group of professional Australian actors to a master class at his theater center in Toga, Japan. To their total surprise, the first weeks were spent in stamping about the stage, putting very deliberate energy into every powerful stamp of each foot. This lower body emphasis was a complete, and initially unpleasant, surprise for the Western actors.

Suzuki did not explain much about what he was trying to achieve, even though frequently questioned, but he did insist that the actors had to learn how to release and express emotions through the pain coming from the hours of stamping. "The body," he said, "knows nothing, carries no knowledge. The body only knows tradition." The actors themselves, when they came to look back on their experiences, recognized that their sense of physical and spiritual balance increased, as did their sense of stillness. Their level of concentration increased, and Suzuki made them vary their breathing, explaining that breathing indexes the state of the emotions, and ends up increasing the actors' confidence.

At the end of the master class in 1993, Suzuki directed an English performance of an abridged version of Shakespeare's *Macbeth* at Toga using the Australian actors. This was essentially an exercise in his acting performance technique. While the actors, when interviewed after the performance, had much to say about their extraordinary learning experience, what interested me most was the transformation in their bodily movement. They performed in an intense, highly focused, physically disciplined, constrained manner, with all lines delivered with strong breath control and constriction around the neck and vocal chords. The anguished delivery of the line, "Banquo's buried!" with the musculature of the shoulder area tightened, was particularly startling, and the whole bodily movement was consistent with what is culturally Japanese.

Unlike Westerners, Japanese make little use of the arms in maintaining the balance of the body, not only in the martial arts but in everyday life. Traditional disciplines of balance are involved, related to sitting on *tatami* (woven mat) floors. The customary way of rising from the floor is to use foot and leg power only, without any assistance from the arms and with a passive but upright upper body. In contrast, most non-Japanese feel they must heave or push themselves up with their arms on the floor or table. In the tea ceremony a celebrant must rise effortlessly from the *tatami* while holding a tray of delicate utensils. In Noh drama, *Nihon Buyō* (traditional dance), and most of the martial arts, the same independence of the upper from the lower body is critical to mastery.

Put another way, the lower body is assigned responsibility for stability and mobility, while the arms and the upper body handle attack, precision movements, or delicacy of expression. How does the upper body achieve this? The key to Japanese upper body passivity and precision of movement lies in the culturally learned control of the shoulder region. Body builders know that control of the upper body comes from the strength of the shoulder area. Professionals who use their hands know that precision of movement of the hands and arms requires the quiescence of the whole upper body area as dictated by control from the shoulder musculature. In other words, the shoulder area is operated very much like the wooden yoke that working oxen are mantled with, where the load is distributed equally on both sides.

The analogy of the yoke helps us to understand what Japanese culture induces most Japanese to do to themselves using the shoulders. Shoulders serve as an instrument of self-suppression, permitting the inhibition of powerful emotions as well as of "instinctive" expressions of anger or rage. The muscles of the Japanese in this area are harder and shorter because they are less stretched. They are kept more in tension, because Japanese spend more time keeping their spines and upper bodies straight, which translates into such behavior as bowing with the upper body kept firm and straight. There is also more deferential standing to attention, more tension in more formal gatherings, and less time relaxing (meaning less time spent loosening muscle tension and stretching of muscles).

Thus the shoulders and their enmantling musculature are the central physical mechanisms for control and suppression of the Japanese body, allowing quick response to commands while maximizing speed of movement and changes of direction. They make lateral movement more precise, as well as being centrally involved in the renowned manual precision and dexterity of the Japanese. Learning to use the shoulder area in an organized manner for self-suppression, precise fitting into the environment, precision manual activity, etc., is a key mechanism that enables Japanese to fit smoothly and precisely into their society. The Japanese themselves are aware of this, since many, or perhaps most, Japanese adults live daily with shoulder soreness or fibrositis (*katakori*), fueling the huge professional massage industry and the manufacture of massage machines, chairs, and equipment of all kinds. *Katakori* is a product of sustained tension in the workplace and in formal social life, aided and abetted by the extremes of winter chills. It is common in Japan for people to massage their shoulders while waiting in public queues or on railway platforms by vigorously twisting the shoulders and head region.

When I ask Japanese where they feel tension, they usually say "in the shoulders." If I ask how they go about achieving emotional control or suppression, the commonest answer is that they use the *sankakukin* (deltoid fascia muscles). This indicates that the area called *kata* in Japanese is actually a wider area than that called shoulder in English. Probably this stems from the more pervasive use by the Japanese of what in English is called the whole musculature of the upper chest and throat area, as well as the shoulders.

One of the few Japanese specialists on movement, Toshiharu Takeuchi, has said that when the Japanese are at a loss for words, as they frequently are, they retreat into nonverbal behavior. He sees all such physical expressions as originating in feelings of anger. One expression for anger in Japanese is *hara ga tatsu* (literally, "the stomach stands up"). This synonym for the involuntary tightening or hardening of muscle that is characteristic of anger shows an interesting Japanese cultural sensitivity to the physical aspect of anger. However, while the English word anger lacks any physical connotation, it does derive from the Latin word *angere*, meaning "strangle" or "squeeze," which was much more physical in meaning.

ATHLETICISM AND RHYTHM

The dual or split nature of the Japanese upper and lower body does not preclude athleticism. In earlier days when most were farmers, the Japanese were avid dancers; it could even be said that ancient Japan was a dance culture. According to ancient myths, an obscene dance lured the Sun Goddess from her cave to bring light and warmth back to the earth. From earliest times, young people gathered for festivals at which they danced, sang, ate, exchanged poems, and later made love. Most villages held an annual *Bon* festival dance in August, when people danced for hours around a central tower on which musicians and callers stood, and they were reputedly very bawdy affairs. Today, most tourist resorts in Japan have a sideshow of seedy strippers doing a poor imitation of a profane dance for tipsy businessmen. At least since the iron hand of Confucian ethics was imposed on Japan from the seventeenth century on, dance in Japan has taken on the simpler rhythms more suited to routine, agricultural lives. Dance remains a part of regular provincial festivals, although most of these today are organized for tourists instead of locals.

During the 1985 Science Exposition in Tsukuba City, a special China Day was held, including a display of over 100 ancient musical instruments found in a 2,400-year-old Chinese tomb. Accompanying this were sketches of wall paintings from the tombs showing women dancing. When the Chinese gave a performance of music on the ancient instruments plus dance based on the poses in the wall paintings, their "un-Japaneseness" was striking. The biggest differences lay in the way in which arms were used in wide arcs of movement, and in the use of long veils draped over the dancers, features that continue to this day in Korean and Chinese dance. In the few sketches and paintings that remain of ancient Japanese dance scenes, the use of wide, arcing arm movements and long scarves seems to have disappeared after the tenth or eleventh century. The more ground-hugging, stability-oriented Japanese dance has been predominant since then. In the eighteenth century, the great woodblock artist Hokusai sketched hundreds of everyday scenes of all kinds of contemporary Japanese movement, street musicians, dancers, acrobats, etc., and in none of them is there any indication of other than ground-hugging movement, albeit athletic and beautifully controlled.

KAMAE *AND JAPANESE MOVEMENT*

The Japanese capacity to move quickly and change direction suddenly (either physically or symbolically) is mystifying to non-Japanese. When World War II finished and the U.S. Occupation began, the Japanese surprised everyone by changing overnight from ferocious enemies to kindly welcomers of the occupying forces. The composer Toshijiro Oka (1981) suggested that the most fundamental thing about Japanese is their custom of pausing and correcting their inner posture. This is called *kamae* (a moment of stillness and suspension of motion). Zubin Mehta, Oka wrote, remarked that Japanese concert halls fall into a hushed silence before performances. This is an instance of *kamae* at work. The prewar *Infantry Drill Manual of the Japanese Imperial Army*, wrote O-Young Lee (1982), stated that the basic *kamae* of the Japanese soldier is "motionlessness." This means, it continued, that "the soldier must remain outwardly unperturbed though inwardly his spirit be overflowing." In business meetings, the silence and lack of movement among Japanese are considered to show *kamae* at work, that is, for as long as they are silent and impassive, they are in the process of adjusting their mental posture. The momentary pause that is typical in Japanese meetings between the exchange of greetings and the onset of business discussions shows *kamae* at work. Westerners might think of *kamae* as the phase in which the Japanese change hats, or masks. That is a reasonable analogy, as long as it is not thought to be a national conspiracy to be tricky or deceitful. It is better to understand that in situations where Japanese are playing a role such as representing their company or country, little if any of their behavior is (or ought to be) spontaneous. Rather, they will be moving from role to role, or mask to mask, each preceded by *kamae* (we might call it internal bridging), during which their external appearance may well be a neutral or expressionless face that cannot be reconciled with the previous face displayed.

SITTING

One of the great curiosities about everyday life in Japan to a Western eye is the ease with which the Japanese squat, crouch, kneel, or sit on the floor. To people encountering it for the first time who were raised to believe that squatting is uncivilized, and that floors are made to walk, not sit, on, this Japanese habit appears backward. Westerners who venture to try it are in agony within a minute or two. Chairs seem a very tangible symbol of the physical comforts of Western culture.

For the Japanese, on the other hand, nothing is more perfectly relaxing after a hard day's work than to sit shoeless and cross-legged on *tatami* in *agura* style. Similarly, when a high school baseball team is getting tense and nervous, the coach will call them together and make them sit cross-legged on the ground. Elderly Japanese women commonly draw their legs up under their bodies and sleep peacefully on long train journeys.

The history of sitting in Japan is fascinating. Most foreigners are familiar with two traditional styles: the *agura* and the more composed, passive, feminine *seiza* (literally, "correct sitting"), where the lower legs are tucked together under the body, with the heels together under the body and the soles showing in back. This posture is also called *kongō-za* (diamond sitting). *Agura*, being a position where the crotch is open, is traditionally considered unsuitable for women unless they are wearing trousers. However, *seiza* only became the appropriate sitting style for Japanese, especially women, in the past two hundred years. Before that, women sat *tate hiza* (literally, "standing knee") with one leg crooked and flat on the floor, the foot under the thigh of the other leg, with the other leg bent up and the knee close to the chin. The *tate hiza* pose was traditional not only in Japan, but also in China and Korea, and it is still seen in Korea today. Why did it die out in Japan?

The reason has to do with the rise in popularity of the tea ceremony and a corresponding tightening of the traditional kimono. In the tea ceremony, both hands must be free to give and receive, and one must be able to make smooth body movements. Neither is possible with the old *tate hiza* style. Only the *seiza* was appropriate to the tea ceremony as it developed. It is also the pose most economical of space, allowing more people to sit comfortably in the traditional small tea ceremony structure. Changes were made to the flowing, voluminous kimono, and it gradually became more form-fitting, with the tightly drawn-in *obi* (sash) that today is universal in Japanese traditional dress.

In the heyday of Japanese mass culture in the eighteenth century, however, when prostitution was legal and great courtesans were often the subjects of popular woodblock prints, ladies of pleasure wore very loose, voluminous kimono. They were frequently depicted sitting seductively in the *tate hiza* position, with a bare foot, or sometimes even an ankle, peeping out shamelessly. The traditional gown of Korean women today is very similar to the old-style Japanese kimono.

Naturally, there are questions of manners associated with sitting in Japan. There is, for example, a pose that young girls find very comfortable, where the legs are folded behind the body and splayed out at an angle with the inside of the ankle on the floor. Very few men have ever been able to do this, and older women say that it is bad manners to sit in that posture. It certainly looks extremely uncomfortable. The position is sometimes called the *karasu* (crow) pose, although in yoga circles it is called *eiyuza* (hero's pose; probably a translation from a Sanskrit expression brought in with Buddhism). Few women sit in the *agura* position, and certainly not when wearing a miniskirt.

In contrast to these everyday sitting poses is the pose used in Zen Buddhism for meditation. Called *zazen* (literally, "sitting Zen"), the legs are crossed with each foot resting on the opposite thigh, and the left leg over the right. Originally, *zazen* came from India. The meditation pose in yoga (in Japanese, *meisōsho*; in Sanskrit, *shidha arsama*) is virtually identical to *zazen*, with the addition of the arms being stretched out, palms open and facing up, and the backs of the hands resting on the knees.

The use of the ground or floor to rest upon is said by many Asians to promote bodily and spiritual well-being. In *zazen* and similar poses, the spine must be kept straight to achieve balance without strain, thereby aiding "correct" posture. The area around the pit of the stomach (called the *tanden* and regarded as the second energy center or *chakra* of good health in esoteric Buddhism) is freed of strain, and breathing becomes deeper and more involuntary. Because of their floor-sitting traditions, educated Japanese have a clear understanding of what it means to center oneself: to breath from and feel the center of one's power in the *tanden*. Floor sitting is said in Japan to calm the constitution, lower blood pressure, and ease tensions in the area of the stomach and abdomen. Some claim that the regular practice of floor sitting also improves sexual virility.

Most non-Japanese, and even Japanese who have grown up in a chair culture, find that they have never used many of the joints, tendons, and muscles involved in squatting and sitting on the floor. When Japanese company employees spend time at a Zen temple as a part of company-sponsored spiritual training, the most difficult task for older managers is when they are required to sit *seiza* when eating their spartan, vegetarian Zen meal. In most such groups, there are usually one or two managers who cannot rise from the *seiza* position, but must be lifted bodily and carried to a place where they can recover slowly. Sitting in the *seiza* position, which is still required in some ceremonies, requires not only the appropriate flexibility in muscles and joints but also a cushioning callus on the instep if one has to sit regularly for hours.

6

COMPACTED LIVING: Command, Compliance, and Self-Realization

Home, school, and company are the three great Japanese "families." The company is the most important and influential of these, a compartmentalized world that young people must learn to adjust to and prosper within. Obedience, commitment, self-suppression, and Japanese utopian values are the keys to understanding life in the company compartment.

As the Japanese "economic miracle" began to be recognized in the 1960s, the Western press and lay observers were prone to view Japanese workers as docile, submissive "robots" who were brainwashed to work long hours, enjoy little leisure, and lack family life. Occasional reports of the everyday life of Japanese concluded that it was only a democracy on the surface but that underneath was a country in which thought and behavior were as controlled as in totalitarian states.

The Japanese love of work has been difficult for Westerners to comprehend. Even today, the Japanese continue to average at least two hundred hours a year more in the workplace than Americans. Explanations of Japanese workplace behavior have varied widely, including conspiracy theories that have every member of Japan Inc. striving for world domination. Other have pointed to the subtly totalitarian command structure, with seniority-dominated hierarchical structures, and fiercely competitive companies. But few scholars have attempted to explain why the Japanese are so docile and easily led.

Japanese are prepared to be effective organizational members by two powerful institutions: school and the organization itself. Each is a distinctive culture into which individuals must learn to fit. They learn in particular the fundamental rules of social behavior, i.e., how to fit into a group; dedication and self-sacrifice; the family-like values of organizational life; *tatemae*; and, perhaps most importantly, how to obey and follow the commands of superiors.

A COMMAND CULTURE

That large Japanese organizations are "command cultures" has long been known, at least since Nakane (1970) pointed out their vertical structure and characteristics in *Japanese Society*. In *Working for a Japanese Company* (1992), I reported that Japanese expatriate managers experience difficulties with local staff when they use a peremptory manner in giving direction or commands, and expect subordinates, especially Westerners, to obey orders promptly, without question. This expectation is not always met, for local Western employees often become openly resentful if they are not asked to do something in a "considerate" way. Japanese managers are more autocratic and coercive than Western managers. Because Japan is a culture of command, there is little room for verbal discussion between superiors and subordinates. In recruiting new staff, Japanese organizations favor candidates with flexibility and a good attitude, since such people will do what they are told without argument.

To the Japanese, obedience has long meant selfless following;

as the prewar ultranationalistic handbook *Kokutai no Hongi* (Fundamentals of National Polity) explained, in connection with serving the Emperor, loyalty means revering the Emperor and following him "mystically." It also said that the basis of the relationship between sovereign and subject was "dying of self and returning to the One." In part, contemporary command and obedience hierarchies stem from the ideology of an Emperor-centered state developed in the Meiji era specifically to promote social order and industrial transformation in which the spiritual was superior to the material, as was the community and group to the individual, and the structure of society was vertical with the Emperor at the top as father of the empire. Absolute loyalty to the Emperor, which in practice meant obedience to all superiors, was taught in school ethics courses and featured in imperial rescripts, in the concepts of the many traditionalist ethical societies developed by both individuals and government agencies, and in the family-like ideologies of business organizations.

Western culture is more generally negotiative, interactive, and persuasive than Japanese. Unquestioning obedience, except in the military context, does not embody democratic and individualistic traditions or fulfill societal expectations of clear communication. The word "obedience" in English connotes a certain lack of moral fiber, or submissiveness, suggesting that those who obey are not standing up for their rights or are accepting second-class status.

In Japan, on the other hand, unquestioning, prompt obedience to commands from superiors is not perceived as having such negative connotations. Obedient people are generally seen as effectively fulfilling their social or occupational role requirements. Requests for semantic clarification made to a superior giving orders are regarded as improper and lacking in common sense. This safeguards the "face" of superiors by proscribing questioning or any other behavior that could imply equality or that could be taken as a "cross-examination" of superiors.

Where does Japanese common sense come from? School life in Japan is the key. From their first days in elementary school, Japanese children are molded into good citizens. They learn to greet and bow to teachers, friends of their parents, and visitors; to clean the school every afternoon; to learn the rules of the school, especially the prohibitions; to fit in with the group; to be modest; and to listen to and not question the teacher. Once they enter junior high school, they realize that elementary school was a benign atmosphere. Junior high school students generally must wear uniforms and adhere strictly to the *seito techō* (student manual). Misbehavior or rule breaking can earn a light slap across the back of the head, rough handling, or "fatigue duty," such as sweeping classrooms, pushing all the desks into one line, and cleaning blackboards and windows. There are many recorded cases of students, especially in martial arts schools, in private academies for wayward boys, and in regular government schools, being beaten to death for ostensible failure to obey or comply with commands from seniors or teachers. Serious misbehavior is rare because of the severity of punishment. By the time they graduate from high school, common sense has been inculcated deeply and most young Japanese are ready to fit into adult society as submissive, obedient new organizational members. They will suppress themselves in the presence of superiors, offer no ideas unless encouraged, and become silent, poker-faced, uniformed, egoless cogs in giant organizational machines.

Rohlen (1974) stated that the goal in early Japanese schooling is "to establish a working social order," in contrast to the American goal of encouraging individual development. In the Japanese situation, teachers stress participation in group activities, compliant behavior, the primacy of the group as one's social identity, and assignment and rotation of duties in the cleaning and maintenance of the classroom.

The earliest training seems to emphasize a particular style of group-oriented compliant behavior, with direct or autocratic command absent. If adult Japanese are asked to identify uniquely Japanese ways of commanding or influencing the behavior of others, they typically maintain that indirect suggestion is widespread. Open-ended questions are used to soften what is implicitly a command; for example, a manager may say to a subordinate who has been chosen to be sent abroad, "What do you feel about being posted to Brazil?" rather than the blunter, "You are being posted to Brazil."

TYPES OF COMMAND

While indirect suggestion and direct command are widely used in adult society, other styles of command or social influence are also used. Persuasive argument, in the form, "do so and so, and you will benefit in such a way," is not uncommon. Social coercion through direct intervention by group members in an effort to change another member's behavior or views are fairly commonplace, and can descend quickly into threats of various kinds, economic in particular, or even outright ostracism from the group or the immediate "community."

Learning obedience involves learning that there are people both above and below one, and that one commands or obeys depending on the relationship. Positions on any Japanese vertical hierarchy have status meticulously subscribed to them, and this usually means some degree of command power in relation to those below that rank, while those below have some, usually unspecified, obligations of compliance/obedience toward those above. Respectful language and nonverbal gestures are also used to reinforce age/ seniority differences. Moreover, the culture emphasizes traditional pairings, such as parent/child, teacher/student, or employer/worker, honored by Confucian ethical values.

Command flows partly from the well-articulated vertical structure of groups and organizations, and partly from a rigidly regulated, structured society. The specific rules for behavior, plus a socially acceptable, well-developed "busybody" mentality that regards everyone's business as publicly accountable, mean that much Japanese behavior is meticulously regulated, both within organizations and within society. Groups, especially those with high status and manifest power, are deferentially respected and trigger compliance from Japanese. Diverse groups are intuitively recognized as embodying the same culture of values and role content. Their familial aspect is recognized, but perhaps most important of all, while people are born and die, groups, organizations, corporations, clubs, etc., are regarded as "perpetual." This encourages a readiness to surrender submissively to the groups one belongs to. Groups and organizations are viewed ultimately as "untouchable," and it approaches sacrilege to criticize them. When the common admonition to promote the growth and protect the survival of the organization is added to this view, the group can be used to justify behavior that might be thought unethical in other circumstances.

Means of exerting influence vary in Japan from subtle suggestion, to direct command, to coercion and threats. One and the same person may use these direct means of influence in different situations. In Japanese business, exhibition by the same person of contrary behavior originates in "role flexibility." This role flexibility allows two apparently irreconcilable sides to the Japanese organization to coexist. One aspect is unquestionably autocratic with a militaristic tone. On the other hand, there is also an organizationally flat, participative aspect, with "low-level project teams with great responsibility, QC circles, assembly and supplier firms doing important design work" (Rohlen, 1974).

SELF-SUPPRESSION AND COMMAND/OBEDIENCE

In the process of learning obedience most if not all Japanese socialization in the family, school, or work organization requires individuals to suppress their own desires and preferences in favor of those of the group, even though those of the group are not usually articulated until a demand for a decision is received. This means that no one in the group can know what a final group decision will be, or when or if it will be made, until the "magical" moment of consensual decision making by the group. This fostering of a sense of individuals being in a kind of decision limbo is likely to produce more submissiveness and, I suspect, increased suggestibility in those who feel capable of "surrendering their will," or at least deferring decision, until a group decision has somehow emerged. Such suggestibility becomes a further factor reinforcing submissiveness and obedience.

A special variety of self-suppression is mortification. This involves submitting one's inner feelings and thoughts to social control, or as Kanter (1972) called it, "the exchanging of a former identity for one defined and formulated by the community." Kanter investigated how mortification works to make communes or utopian institutions more cohesive and integrated, but the same processes are clearly at work in Japanese organizations. She pointed out, for example, that through mortification, "self-esteem comes to depend on commitment to the norms of the group and evaluation of its demands as just and morally necessary." In Japanese companies, this type of commitment is reinforced by the wearing of common uniforms or quasiuniforms such as dark suits and company badges, sharing of the same facilities whatever one's rank, insistence on long hours, which inhibits the development of other allegiances, job rotations that effectively curtail the building of specialist skills, minimization of privilege, and equal treatment for people at the same level of seniority, at least until well advanced in one's career. Such a process strips away aspects of individuals' previous identity, so that they become dependent upon the organization for authority and direction. Mortification thus reinforces the inward-looking identification by the individual with the group, weakens identifications with outside groups, builds commitment to the group, and produces the psychic energy needed to maintain control over the frustration, rage, and resentment resulting from everyday group existence. The similarities between the organizational behavior of American utopian communes and that of Japanese organizations are many.

The "social conditions" that underlie lifetime employment in Japan, historically remote from and alien to those in the West, entail utopian or communitarian values that exist only on the core value-rejecting periphery of Western countries. This is remarkably easy to demonstrate by listing characteristics of utopian commune organizations, taken from Kanter's famous 1972 study of American communes. They are identical to large Japanese organizations in the following ways:

1) Members work to sustain the "transcendent" meaning of the community.
2) Organizations have cohesion and solidarity through commitment. There is no obvious coercion.
3) Individual interests become congruent with organizational interests.
4) Harmony, cooperation, and mutuality of interest are seen as natural to the human condition, rather than conflict, competition, or exploitation.
5) The organization provides material and psychological safety and security.
6) Responsibility and trust are mutual between seniors and juniors.
7) Members "leave" ordinary society to perfect their own existence within the commune or organization.
8) There is an ideal of social unity and a strong vision of a familial community.
9) All life's functions are centralized, coordinated, and combined under one "roof."
10) The commune operates first and foremost to serve its own members (not, in the case of business firms, to serve shareholders).
11) There is a belief that human nature is good but corruptible (as pervasive in Japanese culture as in American utopian communities).
12) Relations with other members are more important than those with outsiders.
13) Conscious planning, control, and coordination ensure everyone's welfare.

14) Jobs are rotated and multiskilling is practiced.
15) Established membership requirements and entrance pro-
cedures exist.

The most salient utopian features of Japanese organizations are
that they are difficult to enter, require a lifetime commitment,
demand personal sacrifices and mortification, provide equality and
fair treatment for everyone within the community, and offer a self-
transcending path of personal development, plus security, identity,
and self-esteem.

JAPANESE UTOPIAN THINKING

In 1974, a series of talks was broadcast on NHK radio entitled
"*Nihon no Yutopia*" (Japanese utopias). The speakers agreed that,
if the Japanese had any utopian dream at all, it was of a house deep
in the mountains, possibly with a pond and a moon-viewing hut.
Unlike Western utopias, the speakers concurred, those of the
Japanese were small in scale. None of my Japanese friends who
had also listened to the program said that they would be attracted to
such a utopia in the mountains. Therefore the question, "What is
utopia for the Japanese?" remained unanswered. However, the
following idealistic beliefs about business organizations and their
operations are widespread:

1) Belief in self-improvement, the obverse of which is dis-
satisfaction with one's self and with one's world;
2) The central role of training and development, and the
rise of the *kaizen* movement;
3) Belief in the perfectibility of man, sometimes called personal enlightenment, through self-improvement as one
of the major staff training methods promoted by Japanese organizations;
4) Self-sacrificial striving and persistence over the long
term for the sake of the "perpetual" organization;
5) Existence of a clearly defined path of personal progress,

along which mutual trust in relationships between superiors and subordinates is highly valued;

6) Organizational membership provides clear identity and (in the case of major organizations) high status within society, characterized by a strong sense of solidarity and shared common purpose between members, and a lack of affinity with outsiders and strangers;

7) Together with competition with other houses, a strong sense of service to the nation (notably in Tokyo); and

8) Individuals socialized into the same values and behaviors (what the Japanese call their homogeneity), leading to restrained, cautious communication styles, inhibition of aggression or direct expression, ability to deny oneself in order to fit into the group, and an etiquette system to fit into a vertical society where one is wedged between seniors and juniors.

This amounts to a description of a system with strong utopian-like values. Japanese organizations function as though they had set up an ideal society where people live in harmony, brotherhood, and peace (typical utopian goals), fostering social unity and maintaining that only in intimate collective life do people fully realize their potential; the primary driving ideal is that of the perfectibility of individuals.

There is concrete evidence of the existence of a utopian ethic in contemporary Japan in men who have become extraordinary commercial successes and thus ethical leaders in the Japanese business world. The first and most seminal of these men was Sazo Idemitsu, founder of the Idemitsu Oil Group. Idemitsu is one of the great heroes of twentieth-century Japanese business, especially for building up the only Japanese-owned oil company, overcoming the opposition of foreign oil companies, and creating a business empire built on practices which, while they flew in the face of contemporary business norms, appealed to aspects of traditional Japanese culture for support (Idemitsu, 1975).

The most "shocking" Idemitsu practice is the policy of paying employees what their supervisors think they need instead of a fixed wage. Idemitsu took the view that salaries are merely a means to support or stabilize one's life. People are given increases according to changes in their life circumstances, such as marriage, birth of children, children's education, and so on. To founder Idemitsu, the basic principle of his company was "respect for people." Since the company was like a family, the first consideration was not profit, but the creation of a family-like world. Believing that people wanted to be trusted more than anything else, Idemitsu banned time clocks, unions, and contracts. He reasoned that if he dispensed with these mechanisms that implied lack of trust, and provided adequate salaries, gave suppliers assurances that contracted prices would be met, etc., there would be room, as he said, for his people to "think of larger things, higher aspirations, such as what they could do for the company or the society." Asked about his philosophy of work-life, Idemitsu often said that the purpose of the company was not to make money but to make people. In other words, Idemitsu embraced the philosophy that the individual who gives himself up to work for the company finds personal enlightenment.

Idemitsu was an unrepentant nationalist.

> Japan is different," he was reported as saying. "... with the Emperor in the center, Japan has developed a family-like society, homogeneous.... Our predecessors never used written contracts; they'd just pat you on the shoulder and say, 'take care of it,' and you'd say, 'OK,' and then you would do it. You'd risk your life to do what you were supposed to do. So Japanese people, even though they may be offered better pay somewhere else, would not necessarily leave their company. To us, the spiritual relationship with our superiors is a big part of it....

The idealism, not to mention the engaging sentimentality, of Idemitsu is obvious.

Fukujiro Sono, founder and president of TDK Electronics, one of the best-performing companies in Japan, maintained a similar philosophy, although he called it Buddhistic in approach. "It teaches," said Sono (1981), "that creative work and strenuous effort are not just means to an end, but the realization of a way of life worth living." Like Idemitsu, Sono emphasized the importance of constant self-improvement. "A company that can educate, cultivate, nurture, and inspire its people to grow is a company that can grow itself." In one of his books (1981), Sono made clear his affinities with Idemitsu, as the following excerpt shows:

> Making a profit is important but it is not the ultimate aim. Character building is much more important. This is what every company should strive for. This is the true way of the company. At TDK we attach great importance to discovering the meaning of work. No longer do we believe that work is just a product or something to be measured merely in terms of time.

Belonging to a younger generation than either Sono or Idemitsu, Koichi Tsukamoto is the founder and president of Wacoal, the leading Japanese foundation garment maker. Tsukamoto acknowledges his debt to Idemitsu in the development of his company philosophy. A key consideration in the company's early days was to encourage the full trust of the workers. So he adopted a number of Idemitsu's ideas. Time clocks were banned. No enquiries were made about people going out during the day for personal reasons. Most revolutionary of all, rather than abolishing unions (as Idemitsu had been able to do), Tsukamoto, who had been having problems with his union, agreed that he would accept automatically whatever demands the official union committee made. The results of these sudden, dramatic changes included a surge in productivity, closer relationships between management and workers, and a strong sense of responsibility among workers that continues to the present day.

UTOPIAS FOR JAPANESE ONLY: THE REALITY OF
JAPANESE ORGANIZATIONS

None of those Japanese or Western scholars who have advocated many "Japanese" management methods as panacea for the West have recognized how central utopian values are to Japanese organizational style. William Ouchi (1981), one of the most influential American writers on learning from Japan, considered the idea that Japanese management has utopian aspects but then rejected it. Ouchi devised an ideal model of a modern business enterprise which he called the Type Z organization. His study of major Japanese organizations and how they operate had a major influence on his ideas. According to Ouchi, these organizations are highly egalitarian, people are trusted to work without close supervision, "intimacy and trust are cornerstones of the culture both in and out of the business setting," individuals are committed to the organization for the long term, and their "feelings of autonomy and freedom make [them] so much more enthusiastic than their counterparts in many Western firms." But, he continued, "The Type Z organization succeeds only under social conditions that support lifetime employment."

If Ouchi had looked more closely at these "social conditions," he would have concluded that, first, the Japanese company has a paternalistic basis, an implicit contract between manager/owner and worker of care from one in consideration of service from the other which owes everything to traditional "house" practices and to ethics of reciprocal responsibility between superiors and subordinates that are still readily understood by modern Japanese as based on Confucian notions of filial piety. Closely linked to this is the obligation on the part of individuals to be loyal to their company, to put the company or master first at all times, and generally to be obedient and deferential and to follow orders. Traditional Japan was a society where houses, not individuals, had legal status. This continues to the present day: individuals are not regarded as having any significant social identity apart from that given by the organization they belong to. Even the recruiting and induction system practiced by Japanese companies has long historical roots and associations, and emphasizes the importance of new membership.

JAPANESE UTOPIAS, PRESENT REALITIES, AND PERSONAL DEVELOPMENT

I have been persuaded to a new view of Japanese utopia, one that emphasizes living in a here-and-now utopia, where the challenge is to achieve a self-transcended state of personal growth that I will call the "realized man." This is a view of Japanese business that goes well beyond conventional ideas of what a business organization is. It ought really to be regarded as a *revolutionary* view vis-à-vis the status quo of contemporary Japanese business and management because it demands a revolutionary rejection of conventional notions of social living or economic or rational organizational relationships.

To most Japanese businesspeople, the views of a handful of visionaries appear quixotic and even repulsive, for the majority of people are not at all idealistic. They do not have utopian visions, or if they do, such visions are likely to be romantic and not centering on the company. It is important to understand the environment of command/obedience against the background of utopian business thinkers, since Japan's cultural heritage has strongly utopian strands, and the struggle for the perfect Confucian state or for individual moral perfection, however expressed, has permeated Japanese thinking over the past 1,500 years.

The concerns of the majority of Japanese are to survive, enjoy modest or momentary success, and pass something tangible on to their children; they can rarely afford idealism. They live within the organization, and their concerns are with the struggle upward. Today, the "average" Japanese businessperson is interested in learning techniques of success in the organization: how others have achieved promotion, impressed their superiors, and made themselves into competent leaders who accentuate their strengths and minimize or conceal their weaknesses. The Japanese business-person knows that today he is unlikely to be asked to work like a corporate samurai in the way his father did thirty years ago. He would secretly like to focus more on making money than on long-suffering self-sacrifice for the company (attitudes inherited from his father), because his prospects for rapid promotion and taking a seat on the board of directors are so poor.

But the values of business society, particularly in Tokyo, still emphasize honor, status, and distinction more than they do money. An exclusive emphasis on money making is still looked down upon there. Thus, intimidated by prevailing values (not to mention severe rates of taxation on personal income) from making money central, the elite Tokyo salaryman is almost forced to increase the valuation he gives to noneconomic rewards like status and reputa-tion, and remains prone in his later years (especially if he has achieved some seniority) to something akin to utopian ideology and the making of occasional visionary pronouncements. When the company has totally saturated his perspectives and self-image, he may no longer be able to say where his own existence ends or the company begins. Such older men who sustain and epitomize the rosy evaluations of the "perpetual" enterprise intimidate younger organization members into continued self-denial for both the orga-nization's and their own (enlightenment's) sakes. This in turn enhances the corporate image in the world of business.

The end result makes the Japanese business elite highly sensi-tive and responsive to their own organization, its suppliers, and its customers, and receptive to information about competitors and new technology. In spite of their environmental sensitivity, organiza-tional members in Japan still maintain their first allegiances to the group, since it is inconceivable and inconsistent with primary group membership that they would have any other loyalties. In such matters, the Japanese business system is still both idealistic and ideological. The ideology is that the company in Japan is not just a money-making machine. It has a soul and high ideals;

employees are surrounded by people who care for them and their future, with membership and commitment regularly reinforced by group leisure activities and meaningful rituals. The converse of this is that the loss of employment and thus of social identity and status is unimaginable for the Japanese.

7

THE JAPANESE TAO
OF STATUS

Social status, not wealth, is the goal of Japanese striving. To be a member of an elite organization and to be respected and honored in the community are treasured goals in Japan.

Kiyoshi Mitaka is a senior manager in the Mitsubishi Corporation. In 1980, he was posted for four years to a European country as the Mitsubishi representative and financial director of their 50/50 joint venture with a local company. Mitaka left behind the big-company, rather bureaucratic lifestyle of a Mitsubishi manager, accustomed to working late three nights a week without complaint and dining and drinking with colleagues most week nights. His new company was small (sixty employees) and entrepreneurial, managed by a profit-hungry expatriate American millionaire and his wealthy English cousin. In place of the camaraderie of the Tokyo office, human relations in the West were cooler, there was far less social-izing, and the lifestyle was more ostentatious and lavish. The American, just married for the fourth time (Mitaka was especially stunned by this), lived in a way that had no parallels in Japan. He owned four luxury cars, homes in Europe, the Bahamas, and on the Mediterranean, a cattle ranch in Australia, and two oceangoing yachts, and he entertained constantly. The Westerners made it clear that they were in the business for the short-term profits they could reap.

At one stage, Mitsubishi was criticized locally for flooding the market with cheap imports, and voices in the media and the parliament demanded the imposition of quotas. Mitaka was concerned for the good name of Mitsubishi, and asked the American to make a public announcement of voluntary import restraint to ward off government intervention. Absolutely not, said the American. We are in business to make as much money as possible. The government has no right to interfere in our business. This bemused Mitaka. In Japan, one does not think about defying the government, or attracting unfavorable attention. But the Westerners seemed to revel in it.

When Mitaka finally returned to Japan, he told me that the opulence and ostentation of the Western lifestyle was the single biggest contrast with Japan. In Japan in 1984, businessmen in elite companies like Mitsubishi thought of themselves as the top of the social heap, but their modest lifestyle was a total contrast to that of the Westerners. Pursuing such opulence in Japan was a certain way to attract public disdain. In Japan, Mitaka added, social prestige depended upon your reputation as a human being, not on your material possessions. This view is still generally held today.

No one can understand Japan and the Japanese until they accept that (except for corruption in high places) it is the longing for social esteem, reputation, and status, not for wealth or material possessions, that makes most Japanese run. As Rohlen (1974) wrote about bankers: "More than material comfort or the power and independence that money can buy, they desire status and distinction...." The Confucian cultural values of Japan imply that people or institutions who have achieved high status have done so due to virtue.

Status and status differences color almost every aspect of modern Japanese life: dress, language, group membership, rank, and, most common of all, age. One's status is an indelible part of who one is, of one's social identity. To have a status that is recognized by others, even if lowly, is enormously important. A cleaning lady working for one of Japan's largest companies finds great pride in the status she has as a member of the company, even though within the company she has lower status than the most junior staff member.

Because status matters so deeply, maintaining status appearances is a constant concern. On construction sites, middle-aged, unskilled men are employed as traffic routers to control the flow of vehicles in and out of the site. Unlike in the West, these men wear uniforms, sometimes with peak caps and braid, making them difficult to distinguish from hotel commissionaires. The dignified behavior of these low-status men indicates how important status is to the Japanese, but it also indicates that their behavior is due in part to their dedication to their particular occupational role. The respect showed by Japanese society generally to people performing clear-cut occupational roles that involve coordination and cooperation with others helps them to achieve status satisfaction.

Learning about status is important. Young Japanese notice how those with indisputably high social status indicate their position by the language they use, the clothes they wear, their personal accessories, the ranking of their company (or university, ministry, or affiliation) in its industry or in the nation as a whole, and where they sit in meetings, in vehicles, or at dinner parties. Other people look up to them and use respectful language toward them, while other great people seek them out. Chauffeurs wait for them when they attend parties at the best Japanese restaurants, or dinner parties with foreign dignitaries. Young Japanese know that they cannot take a single step up the status ladder until they have learned how to speak properly, when not to speak, how to glean what others really mean, and how to be comfortable with more important or sophisticated people. Therefore role models are important.

When the present Crown Princess was still Masako Owada and became engaged to the Crown Prince, she quickly became a status role model for thousands of young Japanese women. Since Owada had attended Harvard and Oxford universities, it was believed that studying at those universities would offer new avenues to status and help them attract more eligible, higher-status husbands. Harvard and Oxford were flooded with inquiries from young Japanese women. Owada's fashion tastes, motor car preferences, accessories, and personal style were all copied as well. The conclusion to be drawn from the Masako Owada story, and there are thousands of other similar stories, is that Japan is preeminently a status-acquisitive society. While much status acquisition is inherently pleasurable, such as wearing nice things or enjoying high-status pastimes, intangibles are also acquired, including honorific language skills, personal networks, listening ability, a reputation for dedication, hard work (or hard drinking), etc. These help one to become more depended upon, looked to for advice, and hence more respected.

The person of high status is placed on a pedestal in Japan. Subordinate people, especially women, tend to toady to and "spoil" their superiors without compunction. The expectations society has of high-status people are of two kinds. They are expected to talk down to those of lower status. In ordinary social life, Japanese meeting others for the first time feel uncomfortable until they have settled the question of who is the senior. Often one party assumes on the basis of appearance that the other is junior, and starts the conversation using a somewhat haughty tone, only to discover that the other is really older. Less ambiguous is the situation where buyer and seller meet. With most markets being buyers' markets, the convention has long been established in Japan that the buyer ought to behave in a superior, somewhat condescending, or even arrogant manner, the seller in a more humble, submissive, service-oriented manner. Small children are instructed by shopkeepers on how they are to behave as buyers. A child who buys sweets at the corner store and says "thank you very much" when she receives the sweets will often be told, "Dear, you are the customer. You don't say 'thank you.' It is I who thank you for having shopped here."

The second expectation of higher-status people is that they should adopt an avuncular or paternal attitude to those of lower status by being supportive and helpful when they are in trouble, and encouraging and motivating them in their striving for achievement. In terms of achieving high social status in Japan, being paternalistic is the surest way to win respect from those with whom one spends one's life in the community. Even in today's excessively materialistic society, the highest respect is often reserved for those whose first concerns are for other people, and whose last concern is making money.

STATUS AND CONSPICUOUS CONSUMPTION IN JAPAN

People in every country love to consume and in consuming make statements about their social status. Thorsten Veblen, the nineteenth-century American social and economic theorist, was responsible not only for coining the phrase "conspicuous consumption" (1925) but also for showing its relationship to maintaining and enhancing the social status of Americans of wealth. Veblen's views on conspicuous consumption help put present-day conspicuous consumption in Japan into perspective. Rich Americans today conspicuously consume large, ostentatious objects, for example, real estate, foreign as well as local condominiums, ski and hunting lodges, chauffeured limousines, vintage motor cars, etc. How do the Japanese compare? In terms of gross ostentation, they do not yet compete. Many have country or second houses, some have yachts, those with condominiums or estates abroad in Hawaii or Queensland are increasing in number, and chauffeured limousines abound but they belong to companies. Conspicuous consumption in Japan is smaller in scale and concentrated more in the area of consumer behavior.

Imported prestige goods have a cachet for middle-class Japanese that Westerners do not feel. Foreignness must be retained for the fascination to work. Luggage, ski- and other sportswear, and motor cars must look foreign, but suit Japanese tastes. McDonalds Japan head Den Fujita has said that even when buying a humble hamburger the Japanese want reassurance that it is a foreign product, so he ensures that his staff uses limited English, such as "one Big Mac, two apple pies," to create a foreign mood.

MONEY AND STATUS

The samurai class of the Tokugawa period set many of the status standards for today's Japan. One of these concerns attitudes toward money. The samurai was taught to look at money with contempt, as something to be handled by (lower-class) merchants and servants. There were solid reasons for this in the past. In the early days of the Tokugawa regime, rice, not money, was the currency, and rice stipends were the hereditary incomes of the samurai class. But the rice economy was threatened by the development of a money economy among merchants in the cities and towns. The Tokugawa government tried to suppress the money economy, with the catch-phrase, "revere grain, despise money." The historical image of merchants in Japan was of people of mean, immoral ways, and it was their reputation for bilking others that reinforced samurai views that money was beneath contempt.

Even today, high-status people in Japan rarely handle money. The only significant industries where business deals are struck today without discussion of money are very traditional ones like *sake* (rice wine). In some traditional retailing also, especially kimono making, Japanese antiques, tea houses, and *ryōtei* (geisha) restaurants, there is customarily neither price label nor menu. Many "high-class" bars only render their accounts the following day in personal visits by the bar manager to the client's office, where a subordinate will usually pay without reference to the boss.

FACE AND INDIVIDUAL OR COMPANY STATUS

Protecting the face of others, as when one pays an account without checking the bill, which would cause the shop to lose face, is widespread in Japan. It is also high-status behavior. Similarly, following the instructions of one's seniors at school or within an organization without question is partly protection of face.

Not only people possess status, but also organizations. Companies, universities, political parties, clubs, government ministries, and so on are ranked by society in regularly published lists. This can be intimidating for members of lower-ranked organizations. Young men who have graduated from universities that are not in the top ten can be snubbed by young women. Hosei University in Tokyo, originally a private specialist law college, has a fine reputation, although it is not in the top ten. A young male Hosei graduate told me recently that young women have rebuffed his invitations after learning that he was "only" a Hosei graduate. Obviously, to many young women, young men are seen not as individuals, but as "branded products." One of my Japanese students some years ago was obsessed with working for IBM Japan. It not only had to be IBM Japan, she said in a sweat of anxiety, it also had to be in their multistory building in Roppongi, on at least the eighth floor, and with views across the city to Otemachi. Those who listened to her teased her for dreaming, but she was deadly serious, and we worried privately about what would become of her if she were not accepted by IBM.

Another student, distinctly mediocre, insisted that he had to go on to study for an MBA at Harvard Business School after graduation. "Why Harvard?" I asked with ill-concealed skepticism. He looked at me with sorrowful contempt. "Because it is the best!" he replied. When asked what he would do if not accepted by Harvard, he stared forlornly out the window as he replied that it would be unthinkable. Life would not be worth living.

Neither of these students sought or dreamed of anything other than high-status affiliation, but both have comfortably survived their unrealistic status aspirations. There are probably two morals to these stories. The first is that youth is a time for most to test the limits of achievable aspirations. The second, however, is that status is so important in Japanese society that its pursuit can be addictive and its loss painful.

When it is recognized how members of high-status Japanese organizations are respected in Japanese society, it is easy to understand why so many youngsters want to become their employees. Such high status will make bank loans, housing, car rentals, or credit easy to obtain. Employment by a top organization changes others' perceptions of an individual so that they behave in a friendly but deferential manner. It is in brief human encounters that one realizes how inegalitarian and hierarchical Japanese society is, how distanced individuals are from one another by the differences in the rank and status of their organizations, and how it is virtually out of the question for people to relate to one another other than through the filters of their organizational affiliations.

8

THE SELFLESS WAY TO SELFISHNESS: Social Influence, Gift Giving, and Doing Favors

Understanding how the Japanese exercise social influence gives important insights into the underlying culture. Social connections and the use of influence are more widespread than in the West. Linked with these are the giving of gifts, doing of favors, creation of obligations, and bribery and corruption at the political level.

One of the biggest surprises for foreigners is discovering the importance attached to the giving of gifts in Japan, and it follows that a major concern of non-Japanese in their relationships with the Japanese is giving appropriate gifts, especially in return for those received. At the same time, one of the most common expressions in everyday Japanese life is *yoroshiku onegai shimasu* or *yoroshiku* for short (I request your good offices or I ask you to do what you can for me). This stock phrase ends any request, for delivery of a product, a telephone call-back, or a favor of any kind.

Why do the Japanese use gifts and stock phrases so liberally, in a completely standardized way? The culture places great emphasis upon the doing of favors, kindnesses, and the development of mutual obligations. This is so pervasive that often people are influenced to do something for others solely on the basis of their desire to be kind and helpful. Naturally, this is strongest among members of the same peer, family, or work group, but kindness to strangers is not unknown. This emphasis on helpfulness begins in early schooling. Japanese children quickly learn to be other-oriented and view effective social skills as critical to human existence. Thus readiness to do small favors or be influenced for the sake of social order or harmony becomes a matter of course for Japanese.

Custom in Japan dictates that gifts be given on many occasions: when visiting someone's home; returning to the workplace after a vacation or trip abroad; at mid-year (*o-chūgen*) and year's end (*o-seibo*); and increasingly in recent years, on commercialized occasions like Valentine's Day, Christmas, Father's Day, Mother's Day, and birthdays. When a couple becomes engaged to be married, the respective families generally exchange gifts. If someone has done a favor, the giving of a gift is a much-appreciated act of thoughtfulness. Traditional etiquette demands that upon moving into a new neighborhood, each neighbor be visited and given a small gift. If it is foreseen that a plan might cause inconvenience to others, visiting them, explaining the plan, and giving a gift is standard behavior. One of my neighbors in Japan planned, quite legally, to add another floor to her house, which would have significantly interfered with the fine sea views that we and other neighbors shared. So she visited each of us, explaining what she was going do and leaving a lavish gift of lacquerware. When major construction is planned in a district, the site manager often visits every resident to apologize in advance for any noise, pollution, or inconvenience, give a gift, and invite those with concerns to contact him at any time. Such gift giving illustrates one of the significant mechanisms of Japanese social harmony.

GIFTS IN BUSINESS

Many gift-giving practices stem from the ancient but surviving practice of giving *o-iwai* (congratulatory money) on special occasions like weddings, the birth of male children, mourning, or completion of a new building. In contemporary Japan, *o-iwai* continue to be given on such occasions both privately and in business, and the business rebate system practiced today is clearly recognized as stemming from the ancient *o-iwai* system. Consequently, it is felt that rebates are means of signifying respect and gratitude for others.

Trade rebates aim at promoting or retaining business, and differ in this respect from margins (which are calculated as a proportion of the purchase amount), and also because they need not be monetary. For example, rebates are given for achieving sales targets, gaining new business or customers, clearing excessive inventories, early ordering, on-time account payment, maintaining a fixed retail price, or not returning goods ordered on consignment. Other forms of rebate are closer in spirit to *o-iwai*, such as those granted at year-end to express gratitude for the year's effort, the so-called madam rebate given to female store managers to express thanks for their cooperation, or those given to express thanks for being given space in a retail store to display one's products. Nonmonetary rebates take diverse forms and can include theater tickets, travel vouchers (sometimes for overseas trips), golf vouchers, shopping or book vouchers, and such items as golf equipment, alcohol, prestige food packages, facial tissues, toilet paper, chinaware, towels, and writing implements.

From being a favor freely given, the rebate in Japan's business society has evolved into an obligation that the giver cannot afford to discontinue. It is the business practice most resistant to the cost-cutting that has been taking place in Japan since the economic bubble burst in 1991–92. *O-iwai* in business, on the other hand, appears to survive only in individual consumer transactions, where it is usually called *sābisu* (from the English word service). *Sābisu* may be a discount, a gift of extra products or of another product, free delivery or installation, or gift wrapping.

RECIPROCAL GIFTS

How do the Japanese handle reciprocal gifts, that is, gifts given as a result of receiving a gift, and what are the rules of thumb foreigners can use in giving reciprocal gifts? The first thing to appreciate is that quite often there is no immediate need for a return gift. If one receives hospitality while abroad, it is safe to wait until the host visits one's home country before reciprocating, or to send a gift after returning home. A second rule of thumb is that the return gift should have the same value as the original. However, when the parties differ significantly in age or status, the value of the gifts can vary. A younger person, for example, can safely give a gift of lesser value, although an older or higher-status person is expected to give one of greater value. Gifts received on ceremonial occasions, of which there are many in Japan, do not require an immediate reciprocal gift. One exception is at a wedding reception, where every guest is expected to give a monetary gift, and receives a gift upon leaving, although its value will be well below the expected average monetary gift.

Foreigners who are recipients of gifts from Japanese should recognize the calculated, business-like approach to the giving of gifts. At the same time, the cultural emphasis on being kind and generous, and the volume of gifts friends give one another out of genuine affection and long-term feelings of indebtedness are at least as great in Japan as anywhere. The Japanese, however, have turned gift giving into an all-purpose social lubricant and conferral of obligation.

GRATITUDE OR BRIBERY?

In most situations, Japanese are extremely sensitive to unexpected meanings gifts may hold. The giver of an excessively expensive gift will be viewed suspiciously, with most recipients wondering if he or she is trying to buy favor. For most Japanese, any deviance from customary practice will trigger suspicion about the "real" meaning of the gift. In actuality, the line between doing favors, expressing gratitude, and outright bribery is a blurred one in Japanese society, in everyday situations as well as in high-stakes political ones. Here are examples of each; the first is at an everyday business level, recounted to me by an American manager friend in a joint-venture company in Tokyo.

> I had an experience today that gave me new insight into doing business in Japan. A lower-ranking woman manager came to my office to "beg my understanding," an expression which I now recognize means, "please overlook all that is happening in reality and let us get away with murder." She came into my office all laden down with little ice cream cakes and a "my-mother-just-died" look on her face. She had to explain another foul-up by her Japanese colleagues. As I sat in the conference room with this gloomy-faced lady, toying with my ice cream cake and a cup of tea, I kept thinking to myself, "Is this a damned tea party or a business meeting? Is this a professional matter or has a dog just pissed in the neighbor's flowerbed?" The sex of the person is not important. As soon as I see a gloomy-faced cake bearer, I know there has been another foul-up.

According to my American friend, he was expected to do the favor of forgiving, forgetting, and forgoing any professional review of the mistakes or problems that might lead to improved future practice, merely for the gifts of an "ice cream cake and a cup of tea." Certainly, the Japanese expectation in such a situation would be that the mistakes be overlooked, on the basis of the personal appeal of the gloomy-faced lady, but I am not sure that a Japanese manager would have been any more forgiving in this situation than my American friend.

On the political level, here is how former Japanese Prime

Minister Zenko Suzuki explained a gift of ten million yen to a parliamentary budget committee in 1992, as reported in *Japan Access* (1992).

> In September 1989, Mr. Abe paid a courtesy call at my office. "I have finally fulfilled my dream of making it to the Cabinet," he said. Then he produced an envelope and said, "Please take this. This is a little token of my very deep gratitude." I started to protest, but Mr. Abe begged me not to humiliate him by refusing to accept it. After he left, I opened the envelope. To my great consternation, it contained ten million yen. I phoned him right away and told him, "That's really quite a sum you brought. I shall hold it in safekeeping for you. Let me know whenever you need it." It was not until November 1991 [after the Kyowa scandal broke] that he finally came to pick up the money.

Asked why he kept the money for over two years and never reported it as either income or political donation, Suzuki explained, "I felt obliged to keep the money in my custody as a gesture of goodwill to Mr. Abe."

Abe had long been a loyal vassal to Suzuki in the political faction he had headed until yielding it up to Kiichi Miyazawa, who then became prime minister. Therefore Suzuki had been in a strong position to influence the appointment of Abe to the Miyazawa Cabinet, and the suspicion that the money was a payoff for that appointment was widespread. In fact, wrote *Japan Access*, "Rumors had it [that] nobody could expect a Cabinet portfolio or a key LDP position without paying heavily the faction bosses and other party elders who effectively controlled the assignments."

OTHER JAPANESE STRATEGIES OF SOCIAL INFLUENCE

The following strategies are used in both everyday life and business to exert influence or engender feelings of obligations in others.

Shame before Ancestors: David Plath (cited in Hamabata, 1990) translated the following passage from an introductory sociology text that describes a powerful influence technique used by parents in Japan.

> ... we often are dragged by Dad or Mom to in front of the household altar shelf [*butsudan*] and asked, "Do you think you can give any excuse to the ancestors for doing that?" The shelf is associated with the household and society, so that rebelling before it is like rebelling against the whole world; and this is why a lecture in front of the shelf has such potency.

Appeals to Conscience: The influence of conscience on the behavior of individual Japanese is powerful. A common saying is: "Even if others do not know, Heaven knows, Earth knows, and I myself know." The Japanese see themselves as *ryōshinteki na minzoku* (conscience-motivated people). Therefore calls to the conscience of individuals can be highly effective among the Japanese, and simplify the process of negotiation. Criminals often confess to the police after appeals are made to their conscience.

Emotional Blackmail: The deep vein of self-sacrifice among the Japanese makes them vulnerable to emotional blackmail. Mothers sometimes say to their children, "If you continue to behave badly, mother will surely die." Most Japanese can be controlled through guilt about making things difficult for those who take responsibility for their welfare. Some Japanese are very much aware of, and resent, their own susceptibility to this kind of manipulation, and in their relations with others are highly sensitive to anything that might be seen as a sugar-coated offer or an attempt to buy goodwill.

The Big Ledger in the Head: It has been said that every Japanese has a ledger inside his or her head into which is entered every favor received and given. The ledger also reflects the connections that individual Japanese have and can count on when something must be investigated or done. Such connections usually owe a favor, so one is in a good position to achieve the desired result without negotiating. The negotiation, as it were, has already been done.

Threats: People who do not accept reasonable proposals or requests or who fail to pay debts, etc., are rarely threatened with legal action in Japan. More likely they are threatened with ostracism: "If you don't agree to our proposal, we'll tell everyone what a rascal you've been, and nobody will do business with you anymore." This is also a variant of group pressure.

Group Pressure: If Japanese are told that everyone in the group, workplace, or union has agreed to a certain proposal they will also agree to it. They will also realize that the truth is that the company president said that the proposal is what he wanted, and thus everyone will go along with it. The twist of the arm is administered in the abstract to obtain unanimous agreement.

Naniwabushi: In Japan, the most commonly used method to resolve or to avoid disputes is called *naniwabushi* and is based on the Japanese narrative chant that goes back to the fifteenth century. The *naniwabushi* as a petition for the granting of a favor begins with a background statement, is followed by a dramatic account of critical events, and concludes with an anguished plea for leniency, embroidered with a story of the dire consequences that will result if the request is not granted. *Naniwabushi* is artful, premeditated, calculated, and usually successful. The more tragic and moving the story, the easier it is for Japanese listeners to forget contractual or other commitments and accede to requests. Listeners who do not compromise or show compassion in such circumstances would be condemned as being cold-hearted or mercenary.

DO THE JAPANESE HAVE BUSINESS ETHICS?

The often melodramatic quality of Japanese life has led some foreigners to rephrase the well-known saying, "That's the beauty of grand opera: you can do anything as long as you sing," to "That's the beauty of being Japanese: you can do anything as long as you are deferential and do favors." For a long time, the successive revelation of corruption scandals in Japanese politics appeared to confirm that slightly poisonous epigram. Human relations are so enmeshed by longstanding mutual obligations and favors that, in the corridors of power and money at least, corruption is no surprise.

Consider the following story about behind-the-scene activities in a major Japanese *keiretsu* (conglomerate). The narrator, Canadian Carlton Patrick, works in the international finance division of a Japanese bank that is a member of the *keiretsu*, which is called M Bank here.

> I know business is business, but things sometimes go too far in this group. For instance, our section was bidding on a project in competition with several American banks, and we were working through our sister organization, the J General Trading Company, especially its New York office. J Trading had a very small stake in the project organization, and this enabled the J Trading people in New York to obtain copies of the proposals of our American competitors. The J Trading men would stroll through our office as though they worked for us, and there was nothing that we didn't share with them. Through them we got copies of confidential documents that told us exactly what our competitors were doing.
>
> Another time, I was told to adjust our standard proposal chart for a Singapore project by changing a few figures to undercut our main competitor's figures in their standard chart of proposal that I was given. I don't know where it came from, but those few changes were enough for us to win the project.

There is no reason to doubt that this kind of cooperation exists in every *keiretsu*, and probably every industrial *keiretsu*-like group in other countries as well. In the Japanese case, however, the pressure to help other members of the group, even when that would seem unethical, is exceptionally strong. Japanese business ethics stress that the primary ethic is to help and support one's own company. If secret information must be obtained to enable the company to beat competition, or if bribes must be paid in order to win a tender or have goods moved, then Japanese will do it with a clear conscience. The reasoning is that failure to do so would show lack of loyalty and support for the company. When I have challenged Japanese to defend this, their answer has been that whenever the choice is between some general ethic and the survival of the company (and that always seems to be the way the choice is formulated), then the company always wins.

When the history and nature of social ethics in Japan are examined, we find that the central value has been placed on selfless or self-sacrificing service and loyalty to the state, or to one's master or lord. There is no universalist ethic in the Japanese pantheon of values. For those who hold a private vision of universal ethics, Japan is a chilling society to live in. The cultural heritage favors a relativistic, situational ethic. In the corporate world, managers of organizations like M Bank and J Trading who are not sufficiently strong or mature to have developed their own values tend to become "yes-men." The organizations become feudalistic in the way they are managed and the way they deal with competitors, making the internal climate of the organization one where "anything goes." While most Japanese business executives who work in such organizations lose touch with their innate sense of what is right or wrong, a desire for inward purity remains dormant and reminds them that, if only they were more powerful or economically secure in the world, they would stand up against up the lack of ethics.

What is happening in Japan today, as far as business ethics are concerned? Ten years ago, if questions were asked about industrial espionage in Japan, people looked blank, denied that it existed, or warned darkly that it was something a "gentleman" ought not to investigate. On the other hand, until the break-up of the Soviet Union, Japan was called a paradise for spies, especially after a number of Japanese were arrested for prising aviation technology secrets out of Mitsubishi Defense Industries. Since the 1991 sale of Komatsu's and Mitsubishi-Caterpillar's technological secrets on the open market, "consultants" in industrial secrets have openly done business in Japan. Some Japanese say that the trade in industrial espionage does not make Japanese feel they are doing anything wrong, as long as they are buying from a third party. Japan's absence of stiff penalties for stealing corporate secrets, plus the excessive competition in the domestic market which makes for an overzealous interest in everything a competitor is doing, can be pinpointed as major factors accelerating the trade in stolen industrial secrets.

The closed, feudalistic character of many companies, especially the policy of "company first, right or wrong," also contributes. Feudalistic companies pursue policies of strict secrecy, even toward their own employees, which are no doubt modeled on the Confucian commandment, "Make the people obey but do not make them understand," and the great guideline of the Tokugawa military government, *"kanson minpi"* (revere the government and despise the people). Such feudal thinking has not died out.

American companies generally have good relationships with Japanese joint-venture partners, but there is also a volume of complaints against the Japanese concerning their obvious interest in "acquiring" (read "stealing") proprietary trade information. The following story from an American manager in an American/Japanese joint venture is typical.

> The most shocking thing for me was to discover, after the joint venture had been agreed to and signed, was that our partner had already secretly developed a product very much like the one we had jointly worked at developing up to that point, and which they planned to have compete with our joint-venture product! That's not all. I discovered that our partner, one of Japan's largest and most respected enterprises, was not carrying out its contractual obligations regarding finance, and polite reminders about their legal nonperformance had no effect at all.
>
> So right in the early days of the joint venture, I had to

reopen the contract and renegotiate it. During this year-long ordeal, I think I saw every face that the Japanese in business can wear. My deepest values were tested: is truth universal? How could I continue to be pleasant when I'm being told that what I categorize as a lie, the Japanese call "face saving." How can I calmly accept the accusation that we— in our role as a partner pointing out the Japanese contract violations—are thereby the aggressors? I had hardly finished this wrenching renegotiation than my partners were crying out for our "know-how." And we are finding out, like so many other expat managers I talk to, that, once you pass on your know-how, it is "goodbye!"

From the perspective of Japanese society generally, non-Japanese must recognize that the evasive, deceptive, information- and trade secret-hungry behavior of the employees of feudal Japanese organizations (which does not mean every Japanese organization by any means) is not representatively Japanese, but representatively feudal. It should also be recognized that Western disgust with corruption in Japanese high places is exceeded by that of the "common man" in Japan. Those whose lives are modest, homes small, and lifestyles spartan hear about sums of money being paid as bribes which are totally beyond their comprehension.

There is a great distance between political corruption and the custom of giving small gifts as an indication of heartfelt gratitude. Ordinary people want to rely not on favors purchased from power brokers but on their own competence. Thus the majority of Japanese are notable for their honesty in everyday life, go out of their way to return lost items, and render small courtesies that make their society work better. Political corruption exists, but on a different plane from gift giving as a social lubricant.

9

THE MIRROR AS FRIEND: Japanese Intimacy and Affinity

What makes for friendship, openness, and intimacy between Japanese, or between Japanese and non-Japanese? Understanding the bases of affinity is the beginning of quality business and personal relationships between Westerners and Japanese.

For most Westerners involved with Japan over the long term, the relationship with the people and the culture tends to be intense. It is one of intense "love" or "hate" (manifested by continual complaints), or both love and hate together. However, the longer one stays in Japan, and there are non-Japanese who have lived there for forty years or more, and a few who were born there and have never even visited other countries, the more likely it is that there will be a more accepting, unadulterated love. There are exceptions, however, especially among those who have lived in Japan for a long time yet do not speak the language and still complain about the people and the inconveniences of everyday life as though they had only arrived yesterday.

As someone who first arrived in Japan in 1946, and has lived there on and off ever since, I have known many foreigners of both types. Some are caught in a time warp, like Gordon Watson, a former Australian army interpreter who has been in Japan since 1945, was discharged from the army in 1951, and eventually became a successful businessman. Gordon is in fact a classic case of the foreigner caught in a love-hate relationship with Japan. He lives in one of the best areas of Japan, is chauffeured to and from the office each day, and is now married to a stunningly beautiful Japanese thirty years younger than he. But appearances are misleading. Gordon's first wife was Chinese, and it was their common alienness in Japan that brought them together. A good businessman who saw a unique opportunity to become rich in Japan, in private Gordon complained unrelentingly and made fun of the Japanese he had to do business with. How did he survive? He maintained his own culture, playing rugby for many years with mixed foreign-Japanese clubs in his area, and later became a rugby administrator. He hung grimly to his 1945 intellectual interests, and when I visited him in 1980, he still only wanted to talk about Winston Churchill and the Second World War, referring often to the leather-bound volumes of Churchill in his study. He lived a fully Western lifestyle at home with few concessions to local culture, ate only Western food, especially steak (an expensive rarity in the early years), and socialized mainly with other foreigners at his country club. Although a superb Japanese linguist, at home with his Eurasian family he insisted that they speak English. As his daughters grew up, they rebelled by refusing to speak to him in anything but Japanese. Today, he continues to dream about retiring to Australia, but seems unable to detach himself from a Japan toward which he has been profoundly ambivalent for forty-odd years.

In contrast, Henry J. McIver, Jr., an American born of a wealthy ranching family, was recruited in 1951 to assist in training the Japanese in large-scale farming, and has lived in Sapporo, Hokkaido, ever since. McIver has a total, unqualified love for Japan and the Japanese. Within a few months of arrival, he found that he loved teaching his Japanese agricultural students. "They were so intense and hard-working but with a great sense of fun; they wanted to learn so much. And they were just nice people off the job," McIver told me. "I soon realized that this was where I wanted to spend much of my life. When I went back to the States in 1968, thinking I had finished with Japan, I got so homesick for Japan that I returned within the year, and have never left since." McIver showed me articles he had written about the economic and productive potential of Japan. He was predicting even then that Japan would become the factory of Asia, just as Lafcadio Hearn had done fifty years previously, although McIver has lived to see his predictions come true. His enthusiasm for Japanese culture today remains unabated. In his early writing he had urged Japan to remain true to its ancient cultural roots and to avoid becoming Westernized. He resented the impact of the Allied Occupation on popular culture and tastes, and today is critical of the Japan bashing that is so common in his native country.

If Watson represents ambivalence toward Japan, McIver represents a deep affinity to and identification with the country. However, the people who feel strong affinity to Japan (and I count myself among them) do not always become as pro-Japanese and anti-home country as McIver. In my own case, I now live happily in Australia, and could not contemplate living permanently again in a Japan that is crowded, frenetic, and lacks the mild climate and blue skies commonplace down under. But if I do not visit Japan at least two or three times a year, I become homesick for it. As a writer/lecturer on Japan, I always endeavor to see it from dual viewpoints.

BASES FOR AFFINITY WITH THE JAPANESE

What makes for affinity to Japan among Westerners? Sometimes there is instant fascination and attraction, when it seems as if Japan and Japanese qualities resonate with one's own ideals or dreams. Many people also experience a strong immediate empathy with the

Japanese. The Japanese value intuitive communication and work hard at empathy, especially with foreign visitors. This often leads first-time visitors to believe that the Japanese understand them without having to say more than a word or two. It is therefore common for foreigners in their early days of dealing with the Japanese to conclude that they are not only capable of communicating well, but also (and more deceptively) that they have a greater affinity for getting along with and being liked by the Japanese than do other foreigners.

Japanese are often ill at ease when they meet people for the first time, until they discover what they have in common. This is thus a third basis of affinity. Points in common can be extraordinarily diverse, from sports, hobbies, and interests, to common experiences (e.g., places both have visited), to friends or associates in common, shared ways of thinking, or common or complementary goals and aspirations. A variation of this can be simple physical proximity. Living or working next to a Japanese person or family is likely to engender a sense of being members of some common entity or group. This relates partly to the next basis of affinity, what I will call collectivism. The Japanese like to do things in a group to a greater degree than other nationalities do. Foreigners who feel comfortable with this kind of group-oriented activity also find their affinity with the culture deepened by their sense of belonging to and being accepted by the group. One of the important consequences of collectivism and physical proximity is the discovery that verbal communication becomes relatively less important in effective human relationships, and nonverbal behavior more potentially communicative.

Foreigners who grasp the giving and receiving of favors, as well as acknowledging and appreciating them, find another source of affinity with the Japanese. Favors and gift giving have such a central place in Japanese social life that people who do not feel comfortable with them as ongoing social customs will certainly be shut out of one important facet of Japanese popular culture.

It is not necessary, however, for a foreigner to have prior

awareness of any of these bases in order to experience affinity. Loryn Farmer, who became marketing manager of the Japanese division of a large multinational tour company in Australia, knew nothing of the Japanese when she first started her job, but very quickly, through observation and asking questions, settled into the post and was accepted by her Japanese subordinates. Loryn spoke of her early days:

> "In the beginning, there was a period of testing and approval, and I knew I had to get full support from my Japanese staff. I think they saw that I took a step-by-step approach and that I worked hard, so those were in my favor. I had to stop and think about everything far more than before. But the big message I got was about modesty.... The modest, diligent, and supportive approach is a key way to secure respect from Japanese staff, and that respect is the number-one criterion for success as a manager...."

Loryn was fascinated by working with the Japanese, and discovered a genuine affinity with the way they emphasize human sensitivities in business.

> "All of us have feelings," she told me, "but from the beginning I felt in tune with the way the Japanese respect and respond to them.... In dealing with a problem or making a decision you will hear the Japanese staff refer to the 'feeling' of a situation. This fitted with my own way of doing things, and has given me a real sense of being at home with the Japanese."

Loryn Farmer is a good example of the kind of person who fits in quickly with the Japanese. She socializes well and feels comfortable with newly met Japanese and other foreigners. While self-assured, she is quick to ask questions about differences or things she does not understand, or to learn by simple observation and deduction how Japanese do things. She then works out what is likely to be effective, adaptive behavior and implements it. People with these characteristics are quick to develop affinity with the Japanese.

BARRIERS TO AFFINITY WITH THE JAPANESE

Japanese culture differs vastly from those in the West. Many differences of background and values mitigate against developing affinity. What are the most likely barriers to affinity with the Japanese? In 1987, an American exchange student in Japan, Patti Namba, undertook research that sheds some light on this. She investigated the cues Japanese use to judge whether people are Japanese based on appearance. Patti herself is an American born of Japanese parents, and she was uncertain about how she would be perceived in Japan. She looked Asian, but was that enough? She assembled from magazine sources photographs of twenty-four different people who ranged in appearance from very Japanese to very un-Japanese, and then interviewed her Japanese respondents about their judgments of the Japaneseness of the photographic subjects and the reasons for those judgments. In showing the photographs, she gave varying descriptions of the subjects, such as, "This person was raised in the USA but has Japanese parents," "This person was born in the USA but educated in Japan," etc.

The findings were revealing. While it is no surprise that the respondents usually judged Asian-looking people to be Japanese, there were other cues as well as to an individual's apparent Japaneseness. The most common that Namba discovered that was critical to being perceived as non-Japanese was *looking directly and smiling broadly at the camera*. Standing with a clearly stylized posture was seen as Japanese, as was having the hair in a full bang or fringe over the forehead, which is common among young Japanese women; women covering the mouth with one hand to conceal a wide smile was also a sure cue to Japaneseness. On the other hand, those judged almost always to be non-Japanese, even if they looked Asian, were smiling broadly and directly at the camera, or, occasionally, were wearing non-Japanese clothing, or were

Caucasian looking. Asian-looking subjects who were said to have been born in the USA of Japanese parents, educated there, and could not speak Japanese were regarded ambivalently. Half of the Japanese research respondents said that such people ought to be considered Japanese (implying that most Japanese would not accept them as such), while the remainder said they would not regard them as Japanese.

The connection with feelings of affinity is clear: the more an individual appears to be Japanese, the more comfortable Japanese will feel with them. The more an individual looks Asian, uses Japanese body language (stylized posture, restrained facial expression, averted eyes, etc.), and dresses in a style that is not incongruous with contemporary Japanese fashion, the more will they be accepted (usually unconsciously) as Japanese. Conversely, the more an individual uses non-Japanese body language, such as looking directly into the eyes of others or smiling broadly, the more un-Japanese they will be perceived, the more uncomfortable Japanese are likely to feel with them, and the less chance there will be for feelings of affinity to arise.

Restrained body language, emotional suppression, and low social risk-taking are typical of Japanese behavior. The Japanese generally feel uncomfortable with people who behave in non-Japanese ways. Hence, foreigners who learn to fit in with and feel affinity for the Japanese quickly learn that they must often mask the overt expression of their feelings. Failure to do this creates the first formidable barrier to the development of affinity relations in Japan. Likewise, failure to adjust to the more frequent use of non-verbal behavior in Japan creates similar barriers.

Affinity also depends heavily on the socioeconomic match between a foreigner and the Japanese dealt with. Marked differences in age, educational level, personal appearance, etc., as elsewhere, make the development of affinity difficult. If one's status is higher or lower, considerable caution is needed in the development of initial relationships. A sense is needed of the type of person being dealt with, including learning the appropriate amount of interpersonal distance to maintain with people of higher status. Touching is unacceptable in Japan, at least until genuine intimacy has been achieved.

GUIDELINES TO ESTABLISHING AFFINITY

What opportunities are there for non-Japanese to break through the barriers to affinity with the Japanese? Apart from body language, socioeconomic matching, trial and error, and empathy, what else can facilitate affinity? Appearance is obviously important. If one looks Asian and dresses in a manner acceptable to the Japanese, many will feel some degree of initial comfort. On the other hand, fair-skinned, green-eyed Caucasians brightly dressed in sports jackets or checked golf trousers will appear too alien for initial comfort. Whatever one's personal views on the freedom of dress or personal appearance, adapting successfully to and developing affinity with Japanese culture and people is only likely when one's own culture-bound tastes are abandoned and attempts are made to blend into the local milieu.

Even more important than how one appears, however, is how one communicates and behaves. Showing genuine interest in others is essential, closely followed by being respectful of their status, title, and position. Being a good listener, asking questions, and showing respect and curiosity about Japan are part of this. Another valuable rule of thumb for first meetings is to behave as though one were dealing with a shy person (whatever their nationality) and wanted to put them at ease. Shy people tend to be slow to warm up, slow to answer questions or start a conversation, expect people to understand what they really mean even if they speak indirectly, are taciturn with people they do not feel comfortable with, and in Japan often avoid eye contact, cover their mouths with their hands, and adopt a defensive or retreating posture.

The most important guidelines for sensitive communication with the Japanese are: giving them ample time to answer questions by tolerating silence, rather than becoming impatient or asking additional questions before they have answered the first one; avoiding critical, sarcastic, or ironic comments about things Japanese; creating ample physical distance (at least 30–40 inches) rather than crowding close and intimidating them; avoiding physical contact; behaving in an entirely predictable, nonthreatening manner; following acceptable formal practice for introductions and formal meetings (there are a number of useful books on this); and observing good hygiene, such as having clean hands, nails, shoes, handkerchiefs, etc., and not coughing, spitting, or blowing one's nose in the presence of others.

Finally, those who want to attempt more sophisticated ways of developing affinity may try: being intuitive; being more group oriented; and becoming a listener and question-asker, especially questions that explicitly invite critical or constructively frank comments about oneself.

JAPAN AFFINITY TEST

The Japan Affinity Test which follows was originally designed to help Western companies identify negotiators who would be effective in dealing with the Japanese. During the ten years I have been using it, the people who have scored high on the test have consistently been people who liked the Japanese and got along well with them. Those with low scores, on the other hand, have been individuals who either had no experience with or knowledge of the Japanese, or, more commonly, had latent animosities (negative affinity) which, however hard they strove to conceal them, were quickly recognized by Japanese. The test determines the degree of affinity one has with Japanese businesspeople. There are no right or wrong answers. Each item has four possible responses. Selecting the large T (or F) means that the statement is generally true (or false); selecting the small t (or f) means that it is merely more true than false (or vice versa).

ITEM	CIRCLE ONE ANSWER ONLY
1. I am very interested in the Japanese and Japanese culture.	T t f F
2. I am as well prepared for meetings as anyone.	T t f F
3. I usually feel comfortable, even if someone quibbles about a proposal I make.	T t f F
4. It is important to be friendly and soft-pedal the "business is business" approach.	T t f F
5. I guess the Japanese would regard me as too easy-going.	T t f F
6. Probably I tend to be in a rush and be sloppier in preparation than I should be.	T t f F
7. Once you have a contract to work with, that alone should decide how you respond to any situation.	T t f F
8. I am a stubborn person who does not like to surrender, even if surrender proves inevitable.	T t f F
9. I often work forty-five hours or more a week and enjoy it, even when there is no particular pressure on.	T t f F
10. I tend to be suspicious of the Japanese.	T t f F
11. I feel comfortable even when a Japanese takes a long time to answer my questions.	T t f F
12. I do not think there is any particular reason to make a deep study of the Japanese in order to do business with them.	T t f F
13. In business discussions, I tend to avoid saying what I really feel.	T t f F
14. I usually feel uncomfortable when Japanese people I meet talk about what is happening in areas I know nothing about.	T t f F
15. Some of my best friends are Japanese.	T t f F

Your Score

Item	T	t	f	F
1	2	1	0	0
2	2	1	0	0
3	2	1	0	0
4	0	0	1	2
5	0	0	1	2
6	0	0	1	2
7	0	0	1	2
8	0	0	1	2
9	2	1	0	0
10	0	0	1	2
11	2	1	0	0
12	0	0	1	2
13	0	0	1	2
14	0	0	1	2
15	2	1	0	0

To determine your Japan Affinity score, add up the numbers of all the answers you have circled. A total score of 26 or more may indicate that you are already simpatico with the Japanese. On the other hand, a score of 12 or less suggests that you are not greatly interested in them, do not have a natural affinity, and/or have too little experience to be able to clarify your attitudes. People with scores between 12 and 25 may either have qualified attitudes to the Japanese generally, be unsure of themselves in dealing with the Japanese, or be unsure of how to read them.

10

NEVER GOOD ENOUGH: The Japanese Addiction to Perfection and Impossible Dreams

Perfectionism is endemic in Japanese culture. It abounds with rules for proper behavior, and there is a general obsession with precision, appearance, orderliness, purity, and cleanliness. Perfectionism also takes the form of a widespread nostalgia for the past, and addictions to work and the workplace.

At 10:00 AM on the day of the marriage of the Japanese Crown Prince to commoner Masako Owada, a school band assembled at the southwest gate of the Imperial Palace. It was scheduled to play the national anthem at 1:30 PM as the royal couple returned to the palace. The bandmaster had been instructed to take no more than two-and-a-half minutes to complete the piece. According to the bandmaster's stopwatch, the first rehearsal took two minutes and forty-five seconds. By 11:00 AM, the band was playing it to within two seconds of the target. But the bandmaster was not satisfied, and it took another hour before the band had the timing at precisely two minutes and thirty seconds.

The Japanese who reported this to me was critical of the demand for precision in a performance that the royal couple would probably not even hear, not to mention the boredom and fatigue of the children in the band. At the same time, however, she conceded that such demands were also very Japanese. "Ordinary Japanese would not worry about such ridiculous precision," she said, "but when we are in a public and responsible position, getting things exactly right seems to be urgent for the Japanese."

LEARNING THE RULES

In springtime, the thoughts of young Japanese fresh from college turn not to love, but to learning business manners. April 1 in Japan is not April Fools' Day, but the day new employees start work and learn to behave with decorum and deference to their seniors and superiors. It is thus also the season for sales of books on business manners. Major bookstores display thirty to forty books on the subject in March and April. For men, the most popular are *Zukai Shain no Manā* (An illustrated manners for corporate employees) and *Jissen Manyuaru Bijinesu Manā* (A practical manual of business manners). For women, the preference is for titles that signify refinement, like *Nikkō Suchuwādesu Miryoku no Reigi Sahō* (The fascinatingly polite manners of JAL stewardesses) and *Hataraku Josei no Hai Sensu Manā* (Refined manners for working women).

Whatever the title, since Japanese business manners are well established and standardized, the contents will be much the same. For example, when walking in the corridor, the young man or woman should: walk slightly behind a boss or superior; stay to the side of the corridor when walking alone, leaving the center for guests and superiors; always be calm and never run, no matter how busy; and never indulge in chitchat with co-workers in the corridor, which creates a poor impression among visitors. The books instruct those escorting visitors to walk a half-step in front, adjusting their pace to that of the visitors. Should visitors be carrying something, offer to carry it by saying, "I will carry it," not, "Shall I carry it?"

which sounds insincere and will usually be refused. When escorting a visitor in an elevator, always enter the elevator first to ensure that the door does not close, but allow the visitor to get off first. There are also strict rules about the correct way to bow and to refer to employees in the same company both face to face and in conversation with others.

In major companies, new employees can spend a week or more in a business manners training course, learning all of the above etiquette and more through constant repetition and role playing. Language training is also extensive, covering appropriate expressions for specific situations on the telephone and face to face, epistolary Japanese for business letters, and the use of *keigo* (spoken polite language). Naturally, one cannot simply take a course to become competent in manners and etiquette. The following letter from a twenty-three-year-old female store attendant, written to a vernacular newspaper, illustrates some of the problems and challenges (Fields, 1983):

> As I am engaged in work that brings me in contact with people, I am always on tenterhooks on the words I choose. It happened when I was being trained on the job to acquire skills. On the last day, as an aside I said, "I was unable to do anything special...." I meant to convey the feeling that I was not able to render great assistance, but the store person did not take it that way. He seemed to interpret it as a protest for my not being taught enough. Thinking back on the manager's expression at that time, I regret that I had not said, "It was great that I could learn many things," but it is too late for me to offer any excuses now. On-the-job training, unlike part-time work, probably carries little expectation from the store of any real contribution, so the trainee needs only to put her best foot forward, but I had arrogantly considered that I had helped out. I did not properly understand my role. I imagine there are many who had entered society and have had trouble coming out of habits of expression of student

days. It is difficult to use expressions that are suited to the moment or take action that is muted to the situation, but I suppose you are called a social being only when you can do those things. I feel I must strive to that end so that I can become a full-fledged store attendant soon.

The strong vein of perfectionism in this woman's aspirations to become a "social being" and a "full-fledged store attendant" is commonplace among young Japanese. The workplace sets higher, more complex standards of behavior than demanded in school or college days. Choosing the language and behavior appropriate to the situation or person is a task that takes years to perfect, but its mastery is critical to social and business success.

THE UNIFORM LOOK

In 1981, as part of its thirty-fifth anniversary observances, Sony decided to phase out the company uniform, a blue and white jacket that everyone from the chairman down to the most junior employee donned each day over street clothes. But given a choice, 94 percent of Sony employees voted to continue wearing a uniform, the main reason being, according to Trucco (1991), that a uniform is a symbolic leveler, bespeaking democratic unity and togetherness. "We feel closer to one another when everyone looks the same," one was reported as saying. Another said, "It means we're all on the same team." Today Sony staff continue to wear a uniform, albeit one that is stylish, well tailored, and carries designer Issey Miyake's label.

Haute couture uniforms are worn by female elevator operators in major department stores, as well as by taxi drivers in provincial towns. It is difficult to find an occupational or common-interest group that does not have a standardized uniform dress: weekend mountain climbers sport plus fours, studded boots, and alpine hats; street cleaners are clad in orange aprons while wielding bamboo brooms; artists and film directors appear in berets and sunglasses; and gangsters with tightly permed hair wear white tropical suits and black sunglasses. In addition, there are firefighters dressed like Darth Vader clones, luggage porters in black French box caps and plus fours, parking attendants as flashily adorned as four-star generals, and schoolchildren in sailor suits.

ELEMENTS IN AND SOURCES OF PERFECTIONISM

Growing up in a rule-rich society is the best possible preparation for participating in a highly organized, regulated, controlled society. The tightly organized society and the excellent preparation of people to take their place in it have led to Japan being dubbed by some who know it well as a truly totalitarian society. Totalitarianism, implying the particularized intrusion of state demands into "private" life, is a satisfactory metaphor for the reality of life in Japan. It hints at the constraints imposed upon individual autonomy and everyday liberties of thought, speech, and action.

The Japanese search for behaviors untouched by rules and prohibitions to indulge their appetite for subjective autonomy, but this is often colored by the search for perfectionism as well. For example, while government treatment of the public in Japan is impersonal, rule prone, and usually arrogant, customer service in private enterprise is tailored to satisfy individual needs. In bars and restaurants, it is common for customers to buy whiskey or brandy not by the glass, but by the bottle. The unfinished bottle is kept for him or her to drink from on the next visit, with the customer's name written prominently on the label. The "bottle-keep" practice is not just good business for the bar. The Japanese customer, who typically keeps a bottle in four or five places, is proud to be welcomed in all of them like a regular, especially when entertaining clients.

Keeping an individual client's items without charge is not limited to liquor: beer halls keep beer mugs; restaurants chopsticks; *karaoke* clubs or bars microphones; and Oriental medicine clinics acupuncture needles and earwax removers. These examples show another perfectionistic dimension: the avoidance of germs and uncleanliness coming from unknown others who might use the same objects. Purity and cleanliness in Japan are closely related to perfectionism. Before entering a temple or shrine, people use running water to purify their hands and mouth. In public libraries, readers are advised to wash their hands thoroughly before handling books others have handled and warned not to lick their fingers to turn pages. When AIDS claimed its first victim in Japan, a woman in Kobe, people from Kobe visiting Tokyo were shunned, and office workers refused to wash cups used by them. The incidence of AIDS has also increased the number of people who will not hold the safety straps in railway carriages because they might carry germs. Emiko Ohnuki-Tierney (1984) reported that the National Institute for Cancer Research wipes with alcohol all the pages of books lent to patients, even though cancer is not considered contagious. The *genkan* (entrance) to a Japanese house, where footwear is removed and put on, is the barrier between the clean, "germ-free" inside and the dirty, germ-laden outside.

Secondhand books, secondhand clothing, and money are regarded as extremely unclean by the Japanese. Some wash the coins and notes they use. One amusing incident occurred in 1982 when a Yokohama woman found ten million yen in notes in a discarded trunk. Prior to taking the money to the local police station, she laundered, and then ironed, every note!

Japanese perfectionism is also exhibited in the insistence on doing things precisely. In manufacturing, the demand for zero defects in products is the most obviously perfectionistic behavior in Japan. The just-in-time (JIT) system of inventory control is equally perfectionistic, since no cost is incurred in storing or purchasing a part until the moment it is needed for manufacture.

The numerous Japanese rituals and other formal events are meticulously organized, precisely conducted, and follow a program like clockwork. A few years ago, I gave lectures in quick succession in Tokyo, Seoul, and Sydney. In Seoul and Sydney, each lecture started late as we waited for people to arrive. None of the organizers was concerned about the delayed start, and when I started to look at my watch and exhibit concern, I was told in essence just to "hang loose." Tokyo was a completely different story. The lecture was due to start at 1:00 PM, and at 12:58 the organizers were on their feet, checking their watches, the microphone, the closure of all doors, and the readiness of the chairman and myself. As the clock raced toward 12:59:59, there was increasingly nervous movement and visual checking. Exactly at 1:00 an organizer was at the podium welcoming the guests and introducing the chairman.

International surveys have shown that the Japanese are the most precise, timetable-driven people in the world. Japanese clocks are also the most accurately maintained. Japanese trains run on time to the second. Add these to ritualized precision and perfectionism, and the result is everyday cultural differences compared to the rest of the world which are tangible and immediately recognizable.

While Japan's smooth functioning as a well-organized society is based on precise plans and meticulous people to execute them, deeper down it also represents a national fear of social chaos. The two great symbols of social order for the Japanese are the *hako* (box) and *tsume* (stuffing or cramming). The box represents the identifying group or frame for each individual, while stuffing represents the capacity to pack as many objects and people as possible within the box or frame in an orderly but tight fashion. The Japanese word *hako* is also the origin of the word *hakobu* (carry or transport), implying that boxing up is necessary to transport something.

O-Young Lee (1982) sees the Japanese cultural tendency to pack things densely into boxes demonstrated in garden landscaping, *bonsai*, the tea ceremony (conducted in the traditional small *tatami* room), box lunches, and even Japanese concise dictionaries, which, although pocket sized, have as many entries as full-sized dictionaries. Perfection in reductionism is a major feature of Japanese culture.

NOSTALGIA FOR THE PAST

A static kind of perfectionism exists everywhere, in the form of nostalgia for a heroic or perfect past. In Japan, this nostalgia is unusually widespread. If Japan no longer has nostalgia for actual rural life, and certainly no wilderness like North America which might serve a romantic retrogression, it does have a robust nostalgia for *furusato* (home town) values. Cleaner than the Wild West and safer than the wilderness, the *furusato* represents small-town bonhomie and intimacy, pure water, air, and food, and innocent, unsophisticated folkways. The *furusato* promises a social framework for life larger than the self and purer than the mercantile corridors of the city.

Japan's *furusato* fascination is the kissing cousin of hero worship. In Japan today two heroes are the sumo wrestler brothers Takanohana and Wakanohana. They speak well, behave modestly, and have squeaky clean images. Although they are too samurai-like to be identified with humbler *furusato* values, they embody retro values and nostalgia. They fit the culture's ideal of warrior heros, with the added bonus of being the sons of a great lord because their father was also a famous, much-loved sumo wrestler.

While Taka and Waka constitute "fun" nostalgia, Japanese nostalgia for the past can be pushed to extremes, as illustrated by the strange life and death of Yukio Mishima, the most celebrated author and playwright of his generation. Mishima died in a prearranged ritual suicide at the Self-Defense Force (SDF) base in Tokyo in 1970. In his own view, Mishima died in order to arouse Japan to its imperial and samurai heritage. He believed that Japan had sunk into materialistic ways and lost its great tradition, and demanded the restoration of the imperial system and abrogation of the Occupation-imposed constitution through a coup d'etat. Laughed at by the media and the man in the street, Mishima was encouraged by some powerful right-wing politicians. When he decided to set up a small private army "to defend the Emperor" and "maintain the national spirit," then Prime Minister Sato and former Defense Minister Nakasone both encouraged him, gave him money, and introduced him to senior people in the SDF. Their common interest was in having the constitution changed to legalize the SDF and allow Japan to possess nuclear weapons.

Although 1970 saw some agitation for constitutional reform in Japan, bankrolled by right-wing groups, there was no resulting public clamor for change. Moreover, Mishima and his private army were given no encouragement by the SDF, making impossible his dream of a coup d'etat. Publicly declaring that he had lost faith in the SDF, he spent his last days finishing his final book, writing his final speech, and tidying up his private affairs. He hoped that his final speech and the ritual suicide to follow would stir the nation to reflection and the recovery of its ancient roots. Ten thousand people attended his funeral. Given the muted public and media reactions, this is curious. Why were they there? Was it a show of support for old values in a world where they were definitely out of favor? Was it connected to his homosexuality and narcissism, values themselves connected through the cult of *bushido* to ancient values and an ideal world ruled by elitist, homosexual warriors? Or were they merely acknowledging the passing of a man "both elegant and brutal" (his own words about the essence of Japanese-ness), someone with a dark side that other Japanese sensed within themselves? Probably some attended for all those reasons, for each hints at the drives within Mishima to realize a perfect but impossible state of being.

MODERN CODES OF PERFECTIONISM

The philosophy of "never good enough" is the basis of the modern concept of *kaizen*, which has in the past fifteen to twenty years become well known as a characteristic of Japanese social or professional technology. *Kaizen* is used today to describe the tendency of Japanese to improve their systems, products, or methods of manufacture continuously. Also in manufacturing, many companies raise awareness of the "three evils" of *muda* (waste), *muri* (unreasonableness), and *mura* (irregularity). In seeking to stamp them out, companies are enlisting their employees in a *kaizen* process that aims for but never reaches a state of product and system perfection.

The promotion of perfectionistic approaches also occurs outside the manufacturing sector in social groups, especially large goal-oriented ones like business enterprises, and in personal life. A perfect appearance, with not a hair out of place, is highly valued in Japanese society. Vanity, and the heavy emphasis upon a perfect, unblemished appearance, relate to the well-known fear of showing one's *abata* (pockmarks, also physical flaws generally). This, plus an emphasis on youth and a strong cultural aversion to skin infections, have made Japan the biggest market in the world for O'Leary's Coverall cosmetics.

National vanity and obsessive perfectionism were behind the Imperial Household Agency's press releases about Crown Princess Masako before marriage, which said that she was two-and-a-half centimeters shorter than the Crown Prince. Anyone who has seen them together knows that she is at least three centimeters taller than her husband. Height was an *abata* to be concealed in this case, and in many others as well.

Another *abata* that "must" be concealed in Japan is *ingo* (literally, "secret language"), meaning argot or slang that some people ought not to use. In my early days in Japan, I was warned by certain Japanese professors that there were words and expressions I should not use. Many years later when I wrote a book in Japanese concerning contemporary problems in Japanese society, I was severely reprimanded by another Japanese professor because I had discussed the sexual problems of Japanese men, in particular *inpo* (impotence). The fact that there was widespread discussion of the problem in serious journals at that time seemed to have nothing to do with his admonition. I was showing *abata* as a professor and presenting a pockmarked, imperfect face to the world.

JAPANESE ADDICTIONS

Addictions are a surrender to a single form of self-expression when life is felt to be a struggle without answers or solutions. Like most people living in advanced societies, the Japanese have their share of addictions: to their jobs, or personal or occupational roles; to other people (especially spouses or siblings) when dependence becomes excessive; to retro values and nostalgia; to obsessive cleanliness; to drugs; and to being a good Japanese. Many of these are discussed in different parts of this volume, but one important addiction not yet discussed is addiction to work, which leads to that uniquely Japanese phenomenon of *karōshi* (death from overwork).

To understand *karōshi*, it must first be recognized that Japanese culture fosters a powerful fascination with people who push themselves to the limit of mortal destruction and death. In the Tendai sect of Japanese Buddhism since the ninth century, there have been just 46 ascetics who have successfully completed the *sennichi kaihō* (1,000-day mountain-walk marathon) to destroy the self and achieve enlightenment. Each of this series of walks is 25 miles and undertaken at night, over a period of seven years. In addition to the nocturnal walks, the aspirant must also undergo a total fast for nine days, that is, two days more than the maximum period for medical survival. On completion of the fast, a final ceremony is held to mark graduation to Buddhist sainthood. What makes this uniquely Japanese is that successful ascetics become the only Buddhist monks officially able to pray for the Japanese Emperor.

The Japanese philosophy of work and human activity is ultimately an ascetic philosophy of the power of the human spirit to endure and triumph. Most companies include extreme physical effort under conditions of limited sleep or rest in their initial training courses for new recruits. Surviving on just a few hours, sleep each night is demanded of every acolyte or temporary resident in a Buddhist retreat temple, who typically go to sleep at ten and arise at three or four in the morning. Those with special duties, such as bell ringing or cooking, may sleep even less. The view that the mind can triumph over matter is deeply embedded in Japanese culture and colors modern attitudes to work. The spirit is important: It enables one to go without sleep, push the body remorselessly, and remain focused even when exhausted. When an individual falters in focus and commitment, the group or superior will make up for it, using coercion and unanswerable rhetoric that work on pride, vanity, and guilt.

Karōshi is by definition a work-related "disease" that is increasing in incidence and has garnered a high level of public awareness, but the Japanese Ministry of Labor still does not recognize that it exists. The approach of the ministry is to look at the hours worked during the week prior to death, and compare them to average hours worked. If an individual who had never worked overtime suddenly began to do so and then died, the ministry is likely to agree that the cause of death was work related, say lawyers working for families of *karōshi* victims. Those who work overtime regularly, take work home, or suffer from high stress levels are not considered susceptible, according to the ministry.

The major problem with the ministry's approach is that in not recognizing *karōshi* it cannot consider measures to eliminate it. Consequently, there are no official government *karōshi* statistics and it is probable that the numbers estimated by volunteer organizations working in support of families are underestimates. Although 2,000 hours is reported in official documents to be the current average for Japanese workers (compared to 1,800 for Americans and 1,700 for Germans), the Japanese Management and Coordination Agency, wrote labor researcher Miyuki Mineshige (*Japan Free Press*, 1991), puts the figure at 2,600 hours, but this "does not take unrecorded overtime or work done at home into account." The lawyer Koji Morioka, in a recent book on the subject, estimated that 10 million Japanese workers put in 3,000 hours per year, or 10 hours a day, six days a week, for 50 weeks a year. In surveys of the physical health of Japanese workers, fatigue is always the number-one problem cited, followed by stress in the shoulder area.

Karōshi has begun to reveal to the world the toll that the Japanese obsession with work can take. Traditional Japanese values make hard work for long periods seem a noble, even romantic, transcendence of self for the sake of something greater. That is not a view to which I can subscribe, nor does it appear romantic to me;

I believe that is probably the case with the majority of Japanese as well. Yet they submit to it, and drive themselves on, since they are deeply if unconsciously fearful of what might happen to them if they were to object. Condemnation as an insincere, heartless, disloyal person coming from those in the workplace who constitute a primary group is often more significant to them than their family, and the danger of ostracism from the group, the ultimate punishment in Japanese society, would be unbearable. This makes a good number of Japanese employees in large organizations look like helpless victims of a philosophy that has veered out of control.

FINAL COMMENTS

Non-Japanese do not easily detect the Japanese addiction to perfection, for it lies hidden in the "deep" culture, and only exhibits itself on special occasions. Throughout this book, I have touched on aspects of Japanese psychology and society for which roots lie deep in and are nourished by traditions of perfectionistic striving for the seemingly unattainable. The handmaiden to this tradition is self-suppression, a factor mentioned in virtually every chapter. Linked to this is submissive, deferential, socially dependent behavior, along with varieties of social influence and coercion, the fear of ostracism, and the inhibition of individuality and spontaneity.

Goals for Japanese perfectionists are diverse. Mishima wanted to restore an Imperial Japan; Idemitsu and his neophytes wanted to create a utopian corporation. Perfectionism is exhibited by each new generation that continues to recreate its ideals of a harmonious, utopian, friction-free society, in which *tatemae* behavior, the concealment of *abata*, aspirations for personal and industrial zero defects, the achievement of high social status, etc., are essential. These all function to maintain a society that is vibrant and dissatisfied with anything short of perfection.

C H A P T E R

11

JAPANESENESS

Attachment to Japan and the intrusion of foreigners have shaped the Japanese identity.

Earlier chapters have described the Japanese behavioral culture that has developed in a stable, monolingual, and monocultural society in which the same information and education are accessible to almost all who live in it. There is more to being Japanese, however, than mastering the behavioral culture. One must have absorbed "deep" or "inner" Japanese culture, the core of which comprises two factors: 1) emotional attachment to the country; and 2) feeling oneself to be Japanese and thus fundamentally different from non-Japanese.

EMOTIONAL ATTACHMENT TO THE COUNTRY

As detailed in Chapter 3, sentiment and emotion override logic and rationality in everyday Japanese life. That sentiment focuses on things and people to which one is deeply attached. Objects of attachment in the Japanese sense tend to be perceived as greater or more enduring than the individual. Obligation is a factor in creating attachment, and is more often the basis of sentiment than a feeling of "love" in the Western sense. Japanese sentiment is usually expressed toward unequal relationships, as represented by attachment to the land, family, the company and one's superiors, the nation, professors, teachers, or schools, and special-interest groups. Attachment to the country encompasses all of these.

Family-like Attachments

In particular, parent/child relationships exhibit more attachment and sentiment in traditional societies like Japan than in advanced Western countries. Japanese children are not encouraged to become socially independent once they reach their teens, although many do so for economic reasons. Parents may begin to encourage independence in offspring in their twenties, but it is more likely that the parent/child relationship will continue with its unequal character more or less unchanged well into maturity, at least on the parental side.

Parent-substitute relationships also figure prominently in Japanese society. *Oyabun/kobun* (parent part/child part) is an old-fashioned term used for relationships between seniors and juniors or superiors and subordinates, with the implication that they are warm and familial. The *senpai/kōhai* (elder/junior) relation is a central organizing concept, under which juniors should be respectful toward their elders (even a one-year difference makes someone an "elder") and seniors should be protective toward juniors. The relationship is clearly meant to be familial. Even teacher/pupil and master/apprentice relationships are recognized as analogues of that of parent/child. In many cases, the socially mandated family-like relationship produces attachment and obligations on both sides that last a lifetime.

Attachment to the Company

For men, the most powerful attachment is the one that anchors their social and economic identity; in other words, the work organization. Of slightly lesser importance is the family and personal life. The maintenance of attachment to the Japanese company demands

self-sacrifice, perseverance, and readiness to labor long and intensively. Even if the object of attachment is threatened and its survival appears hopeless, it is incumbent upon the employees to
strive to preserve it.

The workplace attracts complex attachments: some to the company generally; some to seniors who have served as mentors; some
to friends and close subordinates; and many to the actual place
in which the individual works daily. The *genba* (workplace, which
carries the connotation of the place where the action occurs) has
special salience and power in Japanese organizations. The people
in the *genba*, unlike in Western organizations, possess veto power
over decisions that affect them. For example, if the people in a
production or sales *genba* tell central administration that a goal is
not feasible, that will be the end of the matter. In addition, in the
company, one's *senpai* and *kōhai* are generally all male, as well as
one's *dōhai* (those on the same level of seniority). The exclusively
male work domain is extended by weekend golfing sponsored
by the company and after-hours, work-related entertainment. The
work and social attachments thus tend to blend together in a single-
sex environment.

Company before Family

Of the primary attachments to mother/wife and to the company,
that to the company is more critical to Japanese men because it is
more conditional and commanding. Love of the company (or its
appearance) must be manifested in dedicated, self-sacrificing
behavior. Anxiety and fear are concomitants of such a central
attachment. The wife/mother elicits less attachment and serves
more of a support function. Japanese men who are extremely
attached to the company experience guilt due to neglect of their
families, which is suppressed in part because they do not know
how to balance the seemingly contradictory demands of work and
family. They usually opt to neglect the family because the manifest
pressures and threats from the workplace are so powerful.

The Japanese Language

There is an intimate connection between Japanese attachments and the language of the people. Explaining this requires some historical background. Virtually every educated Japanese today accepts that the language is a composite of words and phrases borrowed from China and other countries in the past 1,400 years, plus novel words the Japanese have devised or invented themselves, upon a base of the original "pure" Japanese language called *Yamato kotoba*, where *Yamato* means both pre-sixth century Japan and the people who have ruled the country since "ancient" times, and *kotoba* means language. In some ways, this view of the Japanese language is similar to that which discriminates between pre-Norman Old English, an almost purely Germanic tongue (which we can think of as the *Yamato kotoba*), and the later heavy borrowing from French, Latin, and other languages. However, while there have been occasional attempts to keep English "pure," virtually no English speakers have any awareness of or interest in Old English.

The situation in Japan is different. Educated Japanese to this day remain aware of *Yamato kotoba*, and there is a consensus on which words in Japanese are *Yamato* and which are borrowed or later constructions. This awareness is aided by the convention of using only *Yamato kotoba* in the construction of *waka* and *haiku*, the traditional poetic forms. Books continue to be written about *Yamato kotoba* as the "heart" or "soul" of the Japanese language, and educated Japanese are easily involved in discussions on the subject.

The preservation of *Yamato kotoba* in poetry and specialist books is a symptom of continuing Japanese interest in the "roots" of their nation. When Western philologists first began to study the Japanese language, they had difficulties in relating it to any other. This was taken by many Japanese to prove that they were a "unique" people, of mysterious origins, who once spoke in the poetic, connotatively rich language of *Yamato* and who, more importantly, even today can take soothing spiritual recourse to

Yamato kotoba alone, dispensing with foreign loan words.

According to Professor Shoichi Watanabe (cited in Akatsuka, 1971) of Tokyo's Sophia University, there are at least four situations in which Japanese prefer to use *Yamato kotoba*:

1. When a Japanese feels introverted or withdrawn, he uses *Yamato kotoba*. When a Japanese feels extroverted, Chinese loan words will be suitable.
2. When a Japanese yearns to embrace something with fond memories for him, he uses *Yamato kotoba*. In contrast, when he brims with ambition or masterful feelings, he uses borrowed words.
3. When the soul of a Japanese is touched directly at a time of inner serenity, he will use *Yamato kotoba*. But his use of borrowed words increases when he thinks intellectually, or distances himself from things.
4. *Yamato kotoba* comprise the complete lexicon for poetry written in the traditional forms, but borrowed words are preferred in scholarly treatises.

To any English native speaker who has written prose, poetry, and "scholarly treatises," Professor Watanabe's distinctions do not appear unique. Prose and poetry in most languages tend to favor shorter, more concrete words and expressions, the active rather than the passive voice, and action rather than concepts or abstractions. Some words are clearly suited to poetry; many are not. Native speakers of any language know intuitively which are which, although few native English speakers know or care if their words are of Old English origin or later loan words.

Watanabe has a special view of *Yamato kotoba*:

> [When] *Yamato kotoba* are spoken from feelings, they are as gentle and soft as mother's skin, as a nipple, or as a mother's womb.... In contrast, borrowed words are hard and stiff [like playing games with men or], having an intellectual discussion ... everyone knows that you don't slip under the bed

covers to nestle against your father's muscular body, but against the softness of your mother.

Nothing in English-language culture can prepare us for such a sexist view of the ancient language that the Japanese seem to hold. The allusions to prenatal existence, or the suggestion that the old language is nurturing, is Freudian to many. (Watanabe also ignores daughters who might want to nestle against Daddy's firm body.)

It seems that the Japanese learn to become highly sensitive to what is happening internally. They put great importance on the feedback they get from their bodies and minds (which may be connected to the interest many Japanese also have in their real or imagined ailments). This makes for an absorbed privacy that all Japanese recognize (at least intuitively) that they enjoy along with other Japanese.

Members of other cultures know what it means to feel "withdrawn" or emotionally down, lonely, and nostalgic for the past; we know that then we speak less and choose to express ourselves with shorter, more implosive words. But, unlike the Japanese, few Western cultures promote sensitivity to internal physical or mental states. Nothing at all in our cultures connects return-to-the-womb–like states with ancient language or culture, or with reveries that seem to stem from a racial or collective unconscious. We think of ourselves as entirely distinct and individual from others. And few English native speakers would know or care if the words they were choosing really were Old English, or some disagreeable, miscegenational, later borrowing.

The importance of such special qualities of "Japaneseness" is reinforced by other evidence concerning the inner meanings of Japanese cultural artifacts. For example, R. H. Blyth, the foremost Western expert on Japanese *haiku*, said this about that poetic form: "[*haiku*] exhibits a certain tenderness and smallness of mind ... [with] a tendency towards weakness and sentiment ... the intellectual element is absent." *Haiku* conveys a strong sense that the poet is discarding his formal and social face and is regressing to a more innocent, less sophisticated state of existence. The same conclusion can be drawn from the following comment on the consequences of the hot bath, as centrally Japanese a social institution as any. The Japanese author, a senior businessman, wrote in a typical way about the rewards of bathing:

> I savor slowly the delights of [the hot bath and] all the things that trouble me slowly fade from my mind and body. I return to *my nonavaricious youth....* In this way, I delight in a complete change of mood. The twists and turns of my thoughts vanish completely [italics added].

The reversion to innocence from an everyday state of interior pollution of some kind is clear here, and nostalgia for the lost days of youth seems connected as well.

Special things that Japanese do in their world—hot-tub bathing, speaking or writing in *Yamato kotoba*, the writing of *haiku*, solitary reverie—all seem connected to youth, innocence, softness, warm naked mothers' bodies, nipples, breasts, wombs, and femininity. Inner states and feelings, inner serenity, withdrawal, other-worldliness, tenderness and smallness of mind, feelings of weakness, and sentimental-nostalgia for the past are obviously savored by the Japanese.

The pleasure and sway of sentiment seem served by these very Japanese activities, values, and inner moods. Looking at the Japanese in private, we can see how they dwell on what is missing, what is loved but far away, in time or space; or we see them enjoying the sensuous delights of nudity and innocence in the bath. We come close here to the roots of not only a sentiment-driven people, but of their age-old hedonism as well.

Sentimental Attachment to Nostalgia

To long for what one is attached to is quintessentially Japanese. It is acceptable to be nostalgic. Japanese are proud that nostalgia is one of the gentlest sentiments in their culture. The prime object of nostalgia is usually one's mother, followed by the *furusato* (hometown). There is no question that the *furusato* is a reconstituted ideal of a "utopia." Since *furusato* signifies a country town or village, in reality those Japanese born in the suburbs of cities cannot claim a *furusato*. *Furusato* remains a highly charged ideal, however, for Japanese. One modern poet spoke for most Japanese living in big cities and separated from their *furusato* when he wrote:

> My *furusato* feels far away,
> So I sing sadly, and piteously lament,
> Like a beggar in the city.

The beggar image reflects both feelings of spiritual deprivation and of shame and humiliation at having to cry (like a beggar) for love in the strange, uncaring city.

Another wrote:

> Alone, alone, in the twilight of the city,
> The thought of my *furusato* moves me to tears.
> How I long, oh how I long,
> To go back to that distant world of mine.

Nostalgia for the old hometown (*bōkyō*) is almost tangible here. So too is an unself-conscious self-pity. And the first poet added to his short verse:

> Miserable as I am, to return would be unworthy.
> What would happen if I set my feet on *furusato* once more?

This poet indicates that he sees through the fiction of the idealized *furusato*. If he did go back, he seems to say, it would be to admit defeat (that is, he was not able to make good in the big city) or he might discover that the *furusato* itself is only a dream.

Such poems show the Japanese dichotomy between what is native and what is borrowed or adapted. Here the distinction is between impersonal urban life and idealized *furusato* warmth and intimacy. There is no doubt that *furusato* (which by the way is a

Yamato kotoba) is semantically linked at this deep culture level to motherhood, *Yamato kotoba*, hot-tub bathing, and *haiku*.

BEING JAPANESE AND THUS DIFFERENT

The Japanese people have long believed that they are the children or descendants of gods, living in a divinely endowed land. In the eighteenth century, the scholar Motoori Norinaga was responsible for resurrecting ancient myths about Japan and the Japanese. Until his time, Japanese scholars viewed China and its civilization as the most important in the world. Norinaga attacked this view, downgraded China, and claimed that Japan was superior to any other country in the world. It was the land where the Sun Goddess was born, making it the fountainhead of all other nations. It had the only classical writings, in particular the seventh-century *Kojiki*, that were true revelations of the gods. It had never been conquered by foreign powers. Its imperial line had been unbroken since the beginning of time. And it produced the world's best rice. These views persist to the present day among many conservative Japanese, defeat in World War II notwithstanding.

With the appearance from the early nineteenth century of Russian, British, and other foreign ships in the waters off Japan, there was heated debate on how to react, since the country had had a policy of isolation from the rest of the world for two hundred years. The military government attempted to promote hate and fear of foreigners by edict. One stated: "We must make our people hate the foreigner and the foreigner hate us." Another said: "Foreigners are by nature clever at winning over the people; therefore, if a foreigner should take advantage at a time when so many are resentful of conditions [there had been many peasants' revolts in Japan] and if they should distribute gifts and favors, it will become a serious matter."

An Expulsion Edict in 1825 once again prohibited all barbarians and Westerners from entering Japan. If a foreign ship was seen, it was fired upon and driven off. Foreigners who went ashore were to be captured and their ships destroyed. The confidence of the Japanese ruling class in their ability to drive off Westerners is reminiscent of the thinking behind the attack on Pearl Harbor.

The belief in the superiority of all things Japanese and crushing contempt for things foreign have weakened but not entirely become extinct in present-day Japan. Although this extraordinarily chauvinistic spirit was temporarily subdued by defeat in World War II, the postwar "economic miracle" and many postwar achievements in industrial productivity and social engineering have provided modern-day chauvinists with ready rationalizations for their one defeat, which they can be prone to dismiss as a case of gross but overwhelming material superiority temporarily triumphing over undying Japanese spiritual superiority.

Ordinary Japanese and Official Edicts

A full appreciation of the Japanese people is not possible without taking into account the peasant, artisan, and merchant classes, who were powerless through most of recorded history and severely restricted not only in personal freedoms but also in their knowledge of the world. For example, throughout most of the feudal period (1600–1868), few ordinary Japanese had any idea that other countries existed, since this fact was, like so many others, deliberately concealed from them by official policy based on the Confucian commandment: "Make the people obey but do not make them understand." Secrecy was, and still is, the fetish of Japanese government, the justification for which is that the people will be more docile if they are kept in ignorance of what is occurring at the level of political policy. Foreigners might wonder why a people already docile should need to be kept in such ignorance. The truth is that during the Tokugawa era and especially in the nineteenth century, and in the 1920s and 1930s, major peasants' revolts were widespread in Japan. Only the warrior class, through the activities of scholars specializing in Western matters, had knowledge of other countries; Western maps of the world were restricted in circulation.

Ordinary Japanese people, until the edicts against foreigners began to be enforced, had occasionally had contacts with foreign ships and sailors, and relationships had been generally good. Sir Rutherford Alcock (cited in Wakabayashi, 1991), an English resident in Japan in the 1860s, was full of praise for the ordinary people, but full of loathing for the military class:

> [The Japanese are] a good-humoured and contented, as well as a happy race ... with the one exception of the military caste [which] furnishes ... swaggering, blustering bullies; many cowardly enough to strike an enemy in the back, or cut down an unarmed and inoffensive man....

It is important for Westerners to understand that antiforeign attitudes in Japan have generally been limited to the official level, usually promoted by the Japanese government to achieve some other end, such as deflecting movements for political reform within the country. In the 1820s, when the edicts against foreigners landing in Japan were being vigorously promoted, some Japanese fishermen rescued by American whalers complained about the falsity of official policies against foreigners (Wakabayashi, 1991):

> Foreign sealers treat Japanese mariners well and without meanness. They most kindly received us.... [They] in no way hurt our fishing.... For what reason then does our government treat foreigners as enemies?

The official policy remained firm, however. In 1838, an English ship, the *Morrison*, attempted to repatriate Japanese castaways from India, but was driven away, and official reports showed the Japanese to be deeply suspicious of the motives of the British in such a humanitarian act. This suspicion appears undimmed today, at least in recollections of the past war. At the Yasukuni Shrine for the war dead in Tokyo, there is a tape-recorded explanation of how Australia treated the Japanese who were killed in the midget submarine attack on Sydney Harbor. A conservative professor, Yasuo Ohara, commented (*Sydney Morning Herald*, 1992):

> The Australian naval people paid great respect to the crews and gave them memorial service even though they were enemies. I greatly admire this attitude of the Australian naval authorities. This should be a universal phenomenon, regardless of the country. But in Japan, such an idea *cannot be understood* [italics added].

This lack of understanding stems from the exclusively Shinto rituals for the dead, which cannot be conceived as appropriate for non-Japanese. Some have suggested that this indicates that Japanese beliefs about spiritual reality and the afterlife are nonuniversal and chauvinistic.

The Ambiguity of the Stranger

It is commonplace for foreigners in Japan to receive exemplary hospitality as a visitor, while being treated by officials or other Japanese individuals in a cold, unfriendly way as a stranger and outsider. What produces this ambiguity? Is it simply a reflection of the difference noted above between ordinary Japanese and the ruling class?

When the Portuguese first came to Japan in the sixteenth century, they were called *Tenjiku-jin* (people from *tenjiku*). *Tenjiku* is an ancient name for India, and signified a remote place, a mountain peak, the sky, and a foreign country. *Tenjiku-jin* were regarded as possessing supernatural powers. One story tells of the Jesuit missionary Francis Xavier walking in heavy snow when he was met by a Japanese who insisted that he melt it because, as a *Tenjiku-jin*, he could call upon witchcraft and black magic.

Historically, the advent of Westerners in Japan has led to periodic rumors of horrors they may wreak. In the sixteenth century, people believed that Western missionaries ate children, disemboweled dying people to make poisons, and could make grass and trees wither at a touch. When Commodore Perry arrived with his Black Ships in 1853, the Japanese were afraid of their magical powers.

When Okinawa was close to invasion by the Americans in World War II, the civilian population was so convinced by Japanese Army propaganda that the Americans would rape, maim, and kill that hundreds committed suicide. Similar rumors circulated on the mainland after the Japanese surrender. In 1987, in Chiba Prefecture, there were numerous reports over a period of a few months that Japanese housewives had been raped in their homes by foreign men. These were eventually discovered to be hysterical fictions started by a single rumor that a "gang" of foreigners was roaming the prefecture. This occurred when the numbers of non-Western foreigners in Tokyo were starting to increase rapidly.

The propensity of the Japanese to believe rumors about foreigners no doubt owes something to their general suggestibility, as mentioned in Chapter 10, as well as to traditional fears of ghosts, devils, and animal spirit possession. Traditional villages used to recognize many types of strangers and visitors from the world beyond, including blacksmiths, carpenters, masons, roofers, peddlers, traders, horse dealers, shaman, priests, strolling players, and so on. However, *tabibito* (travelers) who had no clear tasks to perform were feared and treated with caution. A proverb from feudal days still in everyday use is *"Hito o mitara, dorobō to omoe"* (when you see a stranger, assume you are looking at a thief). The traditional Japanese fear of strangers makes sense when it is recognized that in the past most people spent their entire lives in one village. People within the village were known and had clear-cut identities and affiliations; strangers did not. But there are traditions of strangers who do good deeds. In ancient Japan there was a god called a *marebito* who visited villages occasionally with the intention of bringing them good luck. Even today, rituals continue in the countryside where young men wear goblin masks, or assume the look of beggars, while visiting each house during a festival to ensure a good harvest.

There are also traditions of mysterious strangers passing through villages who do good, usually by the melodramatic overthrow of a wicked landlord or master. The film *Seven Samurai* by

Akira Kurosawa is a famous representative of this genre. In the movie *Tampopo*, a truck driver stops to help a single mother make a success of her noodle restaurant, then resumes his long-distance truck driving when that has been accomplished. Many recent television series have also focused upon the traveling stranger who rights local wrongs and then continues his journey. The appeal of these characters to the Japanese is derived from the ancient appeal of the *marebito* god.

Present-day Attitudes toward Foreigners

To the Japanese, *gaijin* (foreigner) has traditionally meant a Caucasian, and it is only since 1987 that *gaijin* has taken on a wider meaning including blacks as well as whites, other Asians, and Arabs. Nonetheless, when using the term "*gaijin* complex" to mean an awkward orientation to non-Japanese, *gaijin* still means Caucasian to most Japanese.

At different times in the past, the Japanese have acquired beliefs that the distant West is more advanced, wealthier, more powerful, etc., than Japan. They have believed that Westerners are physically bigger, stronger, and more cosmopolitan and self-assured, and that the West differs greatly from Japan in both its culture and its ways of thinking. Given these beliefs about differences, is it any wonder that many Japanese feel frozen by a sense of incompatibility when face to face with Westerners? Among the Japanese, the problems of discomfort and awkwardness with foreigners have been so widespread in the postwar period that the condition known as *gaijin* complex continues to this day.

In an earlier book (*Working for a Japanese Company*, 1992) I reported on two surveys in Tokyo of Japanese which found that a majority of Japanese are burdened by a complex about foreigners that stands as a barrier to effective, clear communication. The survey asked questions about encounters with foreign men and women. When Japanese men talked about their encounters with foreign men, the outcomes were uniformly negative, but they were ambivalent about those with foreign females. In contrast, Japanese women felt less ambivalence, especially with foreign women, and felt attracted to foreign men who were tall, good looking, or "gentlemen."

Dichotomies and Splits in the Japanese Personality

In much that we have examined, a "split personality" seems rampant in the Japanese psyche: sentiment versus logic; cold borrowed words versus soft, motherly *Yamato kotoba*; and *furusato* warmth and sentiment versus city rationalism and coldness. But, in my opinion, the *furusato* "complex" shows that the split is not ultimately about things foreign, but about things strange and unfamiliar. I suspect that the split, which has been noted by the Japanese themselves since the 1950s, has come from the competition between identification with the impersonal organization in the city versus that with the mother and family.

Regional and rural employment opportunities have long since disappeared in Japan. Young men and women must go to the big cities to find work. But that big city world beyond the country town, family, and *furusato* might as just as well be Toronto or Oslo as Tokyo or Osaka for all their lack of familiarity or neighborly friendliness. Although they may live long years in the big city, nothing seems to have equipped many Japanese to put down their roots there and few have made a genuine transition to urban, rationalized existence. They remain polarized people, with their everyday minds hard at work being pragmatic, orderly, impersonal, and rational, but underneath this all, in the quiet corners of their hearts, remaining innocent, hedonistic, tractable, and playful. In the city, they may be ill-nourished spirits, enjoying small fare "amidst the alien corn," but still the "real" self survives and is revived when the inner and outer masks are stripped away.

FINAL COMMENTS

Throughout Japan's 1,400-year recorded history, and probably much longer, the Japanese have retained an awareness of what has been borrowed and what is native. Some borrowings are not acknowledged or admitted (yet); in other cases, for example, rice cultivation (originally from Korea), silk manufacture (originally from China), and the Shinto religion (which stems from ancient Korean animism), myths proclaim their development as indigenous. Virtually all borrowings have been assimilated and Japanized, but the awareness that something was originally a foreign borrowing still exists.

The Japanese have a need to retain a distinct, unique, "superior" native culture that sets them apart from the rest of the world. Like other Asian countries, they have long been threatened by foreign cultures. But they have learned to tolerate conflicts between what is native and what is borrowed, by learning to exist and be productive in two modes of consciousness: one rational, logical, tension-raising, and borrowed; and the other familial, sentimental, tension-reducing, and native. It is the second mode that both engenders and reinforces attachments that make an individual feel distinctly Japanese.

12

EVALUATING JAPAN AND THE JAPANESE:
The Quality of the People, Society, and Culture

Are the Japanese a morally "good" people or not? In one form or another, this has been a serious concern for Western businesspeople, policy makers, and ordinary citizens since the middle of the nineteenth century. Many of us understand so little about them, and, in part because of that, view them as devious and untrustworthy.

How can one begin to answer the question of whether Japanese as a group are "good?" An idealistic response might be that we are all human beings, meaning that no one race is better or worse than another. But experience shows that individual human beings do differ in their goodness or otherwise. I can see only two valid ways to grasp what other people are truly like. One is to view them objectively, as a traditional scientist might, using the best values of one's own culture as the benchmarks or criteria for assessing how good, or perhaps how "evil," they are. The other is to observe the culture while simultaneously noting one's own consciousness, presuppositions, values, and so on. My own approach in this book has been much closer to the second method than to the first. On the surface there do not seem to be any universal criteria of "goodness" to help judge whether a specific behavior in a culture is good or not, and the only way to judge the "goodness" of behavior is based on local values. The same behavior in two cultures could have completely different meanings, while different behaviors could both be equally as moral or humanly valuable.

The American philosopher James Hunter (1983) has developed a set of criteria for evaluating whether cultural elements have universal merit. He uses a number of universal values, including beliefs in freedom, a peaceful society, personal growth, psychological integration, a harmonious balance of individualism and group affiliation, and love and understanding. Drawing on his ideas, I have set six questions to help evaluate Japan and the Japanese. My view is that, if we are able to answer "yes" to every question for any culture, we are describing one that is in good shape indeed, one in which people possess a high quality of humanity. These six questions are given below.

1. Do the Japanese have one fixed, exclusive ideology about themselves and their place in the world, or do they tolerate diversity in ideas about themselves?

In the best of all possible societies and cultures, citizens would be free to believe what they wished about themselves and their society. There would be no compulsion to accept a single ideology or world view. There would be awareness that all ideologies and world views are merely relative, partial ways of stating some "truth" about the nature of man and society. In the worst of all societies, on the other hand, ideology would divide the world into just two groups: the in-group (of "good" people) and the out-group (of "bad" people).

2. Do they enjoy a sense of coherence and order in their lives?

Whatever happens, however tragic and painful, or joyous and exultant, in the best of all possible worlds people would be able to fit their joys and sorrows into a rational under-standing of reality and their own lives. The sense that life or fate is arbitrary or that one is victimized at random would be at a minimum.

3. Do they feel themselves to be whole, well-adjusted, inte-grated human beings?

To feel that one is a whole person, not personally frag-mented or disturbed, and that one's behavior is fully under one's own control, is an outcome of achieving a sense of coherence and order in one's life.

4. Do they feel that they are personally and spiritually grow-ing over time in their society?

Personal and spiritual growth evolves over time as people discover new possibilities within and at the same time achieve social and individual maturity.

5. Do they feel that they are able to achieve a good balance between their needs for individual freedom and integrity and the demands on them for group affiliation?

It is as dangerous to be an extreme individualist, opposed to and isolated from the group (whether family, peer, or orga-nizational) as it is for the individual to submerge him- or herself into the group and lose a separate identity. In the best of all possible worlds, a balance should exist between these, with the individual being a part of the group, yet aware of and accepting inner aloneness.

6. Do people feel their lives are amply enriched through mutual love and understanding?

The outcome of personal growth and balanced individualism/groupism will be, in the best of all possible worlds, enhancement of love, care, and compassion between people, and their insightful understanding of one another.

HOW FIXED AND EXCLUSIVE ARE JAPANESE WORLD VIEWS?

Pre-1945 Japan was a totalitarian society in which people were required to believe in a single, exclusive ideology involving themselves and their place in the world. That society was ultranationalistic and militaristic, in which Japan was depicted as the land of the gods and destined to lead Asia after freeing the region from the yoke of Western imperialism. This rigid, exclusive world view no longer prevails in Japan. Ultranationalism has been discredited, at least in mainstream social, political, and intellectual life. The ideology that has taken its place is best described as a "social contract," or a set of rules by which society generally has learned to operate efficiently. The elements in this social contract, which are absorbed by individuals from parents, the educational system, authority figures, and the mass media, are:

> *social solidarity*, or the feelings among citizens that they mutually support one another, derives from their belief that they share a language and culture and are moving toward the common goal of becoming successful, respected, and significant in the world;
>
> *a hierarchical social structure*, where age is most important in deciding who will be senior or junior, or leader or follower;
>
> *role playing*, where each role specifies mutually agreed-on ways of acting toward seniors and juniors;
>
> *reciprocal obligations* that result from acquiring status and role (employment by a company, for example, usually means a promise of lifetime employment and support from

the employer, in return for lifetime service and loyalty from the employee);

putting the country before self, and by analogy the group or organization first; and

approved censorship, which includes self-censorship, as in modesty, secrecy, and careful speech, as well as public censorship, as in educational curricula and mass media content.

The views in the current Japanese social contract represent a relatively fixed, exclusive ideology that sets limits on the behavior of ordinary citizens, as does the cultural insistence on formal and *tatemae* behavior, indirect communication, and suppression of expressiveness. Although these values are far weaker than the ultranationalistic, prewar Japanese ideology, they are more rigid and more exclusive than those of Western societies. The social contract is for Japanese only. Employment by major Japanese companies is largely restricted to ethnic Japanese, and even Japanese minority groups are, with few exceptions, excluded.

Western values typically encompass relatively fixed ideas concerning social behavior, but there is a much weaker social contract. Social status and role playing are not nearly as clear cut, reciprocal obligation is not an acknowledged need, and no form of self-sacrificial ideology appears popular. As for censorship, any social contract detected in the United States is more likely to contain a clause about impression management, self-projection, and personal public relations than any means of personal concealment and censorship.

Relative to the West, elements of the Japanese social contract appear to be infringements of universal values. The group's rights seem to take priority over those of the individual, with some degree of group tyranny. This is confirmed by the many studies of dissent, oppression, and nonconformity in Japanese society, all of which deserve separate study (for example, Field, 1991; Hane, 1982; Sugimoto, 1983; McCormack and Sugimoto, 1986). Admittedly, however, Japanese mainstream society is characterized by "good" behavior, low crime rates, good public health, etc., suggesting that conformity to the social contract has real rewards for the Japanese, that is, most people feel that it is worth their while to be conformist.

It can be argued from what has been written in previous chapters that vulnerability to social pressure is part of socialization in Japan. Suggestibility and gullibility, hero worship, superstitious beliefs, powerful fears of being ostracized or belittled, perceived powerlessness and dependence on others, and fear of strangers and foreigners are marks of such vulnerability. Due to their dependence-fostering type of society, Japanese mature more slowly than many Westerners, so it is likely that with increasing age and personal maturity (not to mention rising social status, power, and influence), their vulnerability to emotional "blackmail" and the varieties of social coercion is reduced markedly.

Japan is a well-controlled society, and rules abound for most activities. This encourages people to become dependent on others and on groups, because independent behavior seems like navigating in uncharted waters, where one may be criticized for behaving in incorrect or improper ways. But some aspects of Japanese culture also offer acceptable challenges to those who dare to become independent personalities. The ascetic life, and its variants in business and the arts, is one such challenge, providing an independent way, admittedly alien to the West, to become mature, integrated, and independent.

A final question concerning the fixity and exclusivity of Japanese world views concerns chauvinism and the ancient cultural belief that the Japanese are superior to all others. In today's more open society, there is relatively little public display of chauvinism. But recognizing that the Japanese are skillful at concealment and avoidance, can this lack of public display be taken as an indicator of underlying change? In answering this, the first point to emphasize is that generations succeed one another, but the cultural heritage remains. When Japan is threatened, that cultural heritage will be publicly drawn upon again. The second point is that a majority of Japanese, like people in other nations, have no interest in foreigners or foreign countries, except as places to visit briefly in the safety of a group tour. My gut feeling is that ordinary Japanese only think of their superiority when challenged in some way, but that they will certainly then assert it to be true.

Put another way, chauvinism and feelings of racial superiority are potentially a part of being Japanese. I recognize this because, among other factors, I was born and raised in a country (Australia) that was equally chauvinistic and arrogant. Just as Australia is developing as an open, pluralist, multicultural society, so Japan at a slower rate is opening up, becoming more international and pluralist, although not multicultural.

DO THEY ENJOY A SENSE OF COHERENCE AND ORDER IN THEIR LIVES?

Coherence and order are the essence of Japanese perceptions and evaluations of their society and they are rightfully proud of them. A major source of coherence and order is the fact that the country is composed of a homogeneous people, with a homogeneous culture and a single language. It is understandable if Japanese feel unique and different from others in this and if their views of other countries are colored by their own situation and ethnic cohesion.

Coherence and order flow also from the unwavering insistence on harmony as the working principle of social and group activity. Society is well controlled, compartmentalized, and well organized, functioning in a predictable way with the minimum of unpleasant surprises. History, whether national or personal, is cherished, and people enjoy their nostalgic attachments to the past, the land, and social institutions. The streets are clean and relatively free from crime, trains run on time, and orderliness is next to cleanliness. In short, Japan rates very highly in terms of coherence and order. This reflects the perfectionistic tendencies pointed out in Chapter 10.

DO THEY FEEL THEMSELVES TO BE WHOLE, WELL-ADJUSTED, INTEGRATED HUMAN BEINGS?

This question may be approached by asking if its contrary is true, that is, do the Japanese conspicuously have a sense of being unintegrated, diffuse individuals? The answer to this is a resounding "no." They are a socially and psychologically vulnerable people, but this has to do with their shortcomings in socializing and self-management skills. Apart from maturing slowly as social beings, their psychological integration is evidenced by the secure sense of being Japanese and thus different from other people (that this self-perception, and their social skills deficits, can cause some Japanese to become psychologically disturbed when living abroad is a different issue).

The smooth process by which most Japanese mature, the relative absence of abusive or self-destructive behavior, the forming of effective social relationships, low divorce rates, etc., suggest that the character structure underlying the "premature" stage is potentially integrated and conducive to wholeness. Wholeness and personal integration in Japan depend, however, on long-term social or group integration. The discussions of command and obedience (Chapter 6) and addiction to perfection (Chapter 10) made this long-term element clear.

DO THEY FEEL THAT THEY ARE PERSONALLY AND SPIRITUALLY GROWING OVER TIME IN THEIR SOCIETY?

Westerners living in Japan are often troubled by how much Japanese can intrude into one's personal life. Nothing seems private. Many Japanese are compulsive busybodies and take unabashed interest in what others are doing. Those who do not behave "properly" or are noisy or offensive to their neighbors will be admonished promptly. The neighborhood in Japan is definitely not laissez-faire, even in big cities. Many households have quasiofficial roles, which they take extremely seriously, as representatives of anticrime or neighborhood associations. Strange goings-on or the presence of strangers in a town or suburban block will be noted and may be reported to the local police box.

To someone raised in the more anonymous environment of a large city in a liberal democracy, everyday Japanese life has a grass-roots totalitarian quality about it. The state and other people intrude into one's life far more, and Japanese society can feel restrictive, with nowhere to run or hide. The question then arises: can personal growth be facilitated in a totalitarian-like society where personal freedoms are relatively curtailed? The answer lies in the understanding of personal growth, and of personal maturity as the culmination of such growth. My answer is that someone is personally growing and developing when they are seeking to:

1. *think in a constructive and nondestructive manner*;
2. *choose to hold positive attitudes* to their lives and other people, whatever the external restrictions placed upon them;
3. *take responsibility* for the quality of their lives, not blaming others or playing victim;
4. *are inwardly calm* whatever is happening;
5. *have effective emotional and expressive lives*, which necessarily means using restraint and suppression of emotion according to commonsense judgment of situations;
6. *enjoy close and intimate relationships* with select others; and
7. *recognize that nothing is unthinkable*, that nothing is ultimately taboo or to be avoided if one wishes to grow as a person.

If this view of personal growth is accepted, then it is obvious that there is just as much opportunity for personal growth in Japan's restricted, highly organized, controlled, densely packed society as there is in wide, diffusely populated, less intensively organized societies like the United States, Canada, or Australia.

Points throughout this book have described how the Japanese are able to achieve inner privacy in their group-oriented society.

As gullible as they may be, they are protected from deception most of the time by socializing only with people they know well, trust, and have long-term relationships with. As part of the everyday wisdom of the culture, they are taught to be cautious with strangers and nonintimates, not to wear their hearts on their sleeves, to be suspicious of fine words, and not to take words at face value. These lessons eventually stick. This circumspection does not inhibit personal growth in a small space, however. Conceivably, such restriction may promote personal growth and acceptance of life's limitations upon a burgeoning, infantile ego.

Chapter 5 described how integrated into Japanese culture the notions of personal balance and harmony are, in both the emphasis on bodily balance and the pervasive ideal of harmony in human relations. These characteristics, aided by the general social injunction against aggressive thoughts and behavior, foster inner calm and support personal growth.

DO THEY FEEL ABLE TO ACHIEVE A GOOD BALANCE BETWEEN THEIR NEEDS FOR INDIVIDUAL FREEDOM AND INTEGRITY AND THE DEMANDS ON THEM FOR GROUP MEMBERSHIP AND AFFILIATION?

A common criticism is that the Japanese are too group-oriented and not sufficiently individualistic. This is usually expressed by: "They cannot act on their own initiative." "They cannot do anything on their own. For instance, at lunchtime, they all go out together, and no one will take an elevator unless everyone in the group can squeeze in." "They are incapable of independent thought, even on commonplace matters." "They behave like sheep when traveling in a group. Even when a choice of meals is provided, everyone usually eats the same meal." "They are submissive robots without minds of their own." However, it should be clear that what Japanese say or do in public does not necessarily reflect their inner thoughts or temperament. They may be chronic conformists, or they may be acting out of fear of criticism by other group members.

Overt behavior does not necessarily reveal much about the inner dimensions of attitude, particularly in the case of the Japanese.

How then can this criterion of group versus individual affiliation be evaluated? The first point to recognize is that when Hunter (1983) wrote about this question, he was concerned that individuals who "submerged their identities in a group" were exposing themselves to illicit manipulation and coercion. This might mean, for example, being coerced into doing something immoral, illegal, or life-threatening, becoming the dupe of a leader or group, or having one's personal integrity violated, so that one's life and life chances were seriously diminished in quality and potential.

The dangers of excessive group dependence leading to generally threatening consequences in Japan arise in a limited number of circumstances. One of the most common is extreme overwork as a result of group pressure leading eventually to *karōshi* (death from overwork, as discussed in Chapter 6). The *karōshi* process begins with a romanticized view of work as a struggle between man's higher and lower selves, accompanied by a demand for exceedingly unreasonable hours of work, abetted by a self-sacrificial attitude that is culturally determined, and sustained by powerful sanctions in the culture against complaining. The display of a lack of will to work, a proneness to complain, or unwillingness to follow rules is seen as profoundly unmanly in Japan; vulnerability to criticism on such scores simply reinforces self-sacrificial, and perhaps ultimately self-destroying, attitudes. This is a critical weakness in Japanese industrial society from the viewpoint of human rights and health.

An alternative viewpoint is that work in Japanese enterprises is colored by the traditions of Buddhist ascetic life, where individuals push themselves to the limit to achieve self-realization. In the idealistic ideologies of work formulated by Sazo Idemitsu and his imitators, this ascetic element is very close to the surface. Idemitsu saw work as a "means to the end of making a man," and most Japanese managers share roughly similar views. In this view, if one happens to die in the process of struggling to achieve a goal of self-realization, it is a chance that all ascetics must take, and the result is relatively unimportant since the next incarnation will be as a somewhat more advanced soul.

This is a suitably ennobling viewpoint. Its flaw lies in the fact that ascetics choose their way and are in charge of what they do all the time. When they push themselves to the brink of death, no one is there urging them on, mocking their lack of manhood, or threatening implicitly that their job is in danger. The ascetic has left society as we know it. The analogy urged upon Japanese society by industrialists like Idemitsu, namely, that workers are spiritual warriors involved in the supreme task of realizing their true spirituality, is therefore manifestly false. Few workers choose an ascetic-like approach to their work. Most would prefer that they did not have to behave as though the workplace were a spiritual training ground, to which home and personal life were subordinated. But Japanese business and bureaucratic society have made the rules. Male pride is also involved. Young men do not understand that they are mortal, and a few believe that they may just be able to achieve the impossible. They may also, in their naivete, have little real choice, especially because business and bureaucratic work life are romanticized in Japanese culture. Only in business and the bureaucracies can one achieve the high status and the respect of one's fellows that give completion and closure to Japanese social existence.

There is another danger in the ascetic analogy: It suggests that the "aspirant" need only be inward-oriented and self-absorbed. Questions of the moral or absolute value of what he or she does do not arise, or are seen as inappropriate. The encompassing organization, already thought of as eternal and for all time (unlike the aspirant), is assumed also to be ethically omniscient. It is therefore all too easy to conclude that "we can safely leave questions of greater moment to the wisdom of the managers and the good sense of the organization."

The observation in Chapter 6 that Japanese employees judge the ethical quality of their behavior solely on whether it contributes to the survival and growth of the enterprise, and not on the basis of any universal ethic, also indicates how such an autistic orientation must eventually corrode the ethical sensibilities of many Japanese. There is other evidence to support that view in this book. Moreover, within Japanese organizations, the consensus decision-making style also presents the danger that single individuals come to feel powerless to influence decisions, or to bring about needed changes in the organization. Decisions once made become political icons that only the foolish would attempt to modify, due to the face and pride of people who have put their seals on them. In addition, the emphasis of the work ethic in Japanese companies is on the individual coming to believe that it is not the organization that must change, but oneself. In making a commitment to the organization, the employee also offers himself as a tabula rasa on which superiors can engrave what they will. The "inner meaning" of self-sacrifice, acceptance of ambiguity, and acceptance of mortification must be learned.

What finally can be said in summary about the balance between group dependence and individual autonomy? In everyday life, the apparent dependence of individuals on the groups to which they belong does not constitute an identity loss that could threaten the individual. But in the work world, because occupational mobility is rare, there is more readiness to tolerate the existing circumstances. Often employees and managers who are shut off from the rest of the world become ethically desensitized, and occasionally this has outcomes that are life-threatening.

DO PEOPLE FEEL THEIR LIVES ARE AMPLY ENRICHED THROUGH LOVE AND UNDERSTANDING?

Words like "love" and "understanding" suffer greatly in translation. They carry a load of surplus meaning that can be purely cultural. In the West, "love" has heavy overtones of heterosexual romance, expressive body language, and displays of physical affection. None of this translates easily into Japanese, either linguistically or culturally. Herbert Passin (1980), in an amusing essay called "I Love You," showed how the word "love," when borrowed by the Japanese, has been trivialized and possibly debased in ways we could not anticipate. "Understanding," seemingly more cognitive, is less troublesome. Japanese has several words to do the job of translating it.

Translation and culture apart, a second problem in talking about love and understanding is the Japanese preference for circumlocution and indirect speech. If one asked as though doing a market survey, "To what extent is your life enriched through love and understanding in your relationships with others?" the answer would probably be that the question is ridiculous. If a Japanese is in a relationship where he or she feels generally self-sacrificing, it would probably not matter if the other party loved or understood him or her. It would be enough to be permitted to be of service.

Japanese shyness with strangers might affect Western judgments about their capacity for love and understanding. Shyness is notorious among the young, who avert their eyes, put hands over mouths, and manage to look thoroughly awkward with strangers. Since shyness is positively valued, shy people are not criticized for social incompetence but applauded for greater innocence and for being less socially "sophisticated." This means that the opportunities for shy Japanese to enter intimate relationships are actually greater than for shy Westerners.

What Westerners have to be careful of is judging the Japanese on the basis of their public, *tatemae* behavior. Anyone playing an official, formal role will look cold and not very human, and not capable of much love and understanding. And, since a lot of Japanese do feel uncomfortable with foreigners (even though it may not appear so), their capacity for loving and understanding may not be apparent.

Love and understanding are at the heart of personal growth. Since I have already concluded that personal growth is a reality for Japanese, notwithstanding their close-knit society, I see the Japanese generally as a loving, understanding people. But it is a Japanese form of love and understanding. Service to others, often submissive and selfless (like the *marebito* god's visits), is at the heart of it. Tolerating deviance in and giving space to others to help them to grow, which is so much a part of educational philosophy in Japan, is also of major importance. Even the ideal of the realized man, whether in business like Idemitsu or in the ascetic life of a Buddhist monk, can be seen as extremities of the highest order of love and understanding, where man is allowed to stretch himself to become a "Buddha" through ascetic practice.

FINAL COMMENTS

Japanese private lives are generally characterized by interpersonal intimacy, compassion, tolerance, and kindness to one another. There is little use for romance-tinged expressions of "love." Public lives, however, exhibit more complexity. There is a paternalism that provides emotional and economic security to a greater degree than in the West side by side with cold rationality, an authoritarian command system, and low tolerance for behavior that does not follow expected mores and values.

Japanese are proud and moderately nationalistic, more chauvinistic and exclusive, and less tolerant of political dissent or radicalism than, for example, Americans. On the other hand, theirs is a superbly ordered, secure, well-managed, coherent society, perceptions which the people themselves share and feel are positive rewards for being Japanese. Within the explicit rules and guidelines of the society, individuals show a high degree of suggestibility and personal vulnerability to social influence, making social change particularly easy to "engineer." This is facilitated by the greater omnipresence of "behavioral monitors" (busybodies, moral authorities, self-righteous seniors, etc.). Notwithstanding the prevalence of social demands for conformist behavior and the frequent intrusion of others into their private lives, they enjoy at least as much opportunity for personal growth and inner well-being as people in other nations do.

There are two significant universalistic concerns in Japanese organizational life. One is that the extremity of demands for overwork can sometimes lead to *karōshi*, or death from overwork. This is reinforced by a specious philosophy of asceticism, borrowed from Buddhist monastic life, which accentuates social and emotional pressure upon individuals to sacrifice themselves for organizations as though they were quasireligious bodies. The second concern is the lack of universal ethical standards, the gestation and growth of which are suppressed by the consistent, overwhelming demand for a situational ethic or for loyalty to the immediate group or organization as the primary determinant of ethical behavior.

13

THE AUM SHINRIKYŌ AFFAIR, JAPANESE NATIONAL CHAR-ACTER, AND THE FUTURE OF JAPANESE SOCIETY

Not long after finishing this book, a series of events occurred in Japan in 1995 which caused many people to rethink their ideas about the Japanese people and society. These events were not only "apocalyptic" in their impact, they were a watershed in the evolution of Japanese society. This additional chapter, in examining the rise and fall of the Aum Shinrikyō movement, shows how the year 1995 lead to the first great national experience of the Japanese people since their defeat in 1945, which in the process revealed more of the ways of thinking of the Japanese. It also reinforced many of the points of analysis presented in earlier chapters.

EVENTS OF 1995 IN CONTEXT

1995 will remain as unforgettable and critical a year for the Japanese as 1945, the year of surrender in World War II. The Great Hanshin Earthquake on January 17 in which 6,000 were killed, 25,000 injured, and 300,000 rendered homeless was devastating. This was followed by sarin gas attacks first in the Tokyo subway system in March, in which 12 people were killed and 6,000 injured, and then by further incidents in which nerve gas was discovered in major Tokyo stations in June. The Japanese, once proud of their earthquake readiness and crime-free urban environment, were robbed all at once of innocence, peace of mind, and national pride. Whatever the Japanese might have thought of their country before, 1995 destroyed any last pretensions that it was "the land of the gods." Trust in society and its institutions was dealt the most crippling blow since 1945. If trust and security were lost, some wondered if there was any point in continuing to be "good" conformists. Were the rewards for lifelong obedience and conformity disappearing?

Immediately after the earthquake and the sarin attacks, voters in the two biggest cities of Tokyo and Osaka elected as governors not members of established political parties but professional comedians who also happened to be independent, unaffiliated politicians. Was the dire irony of their lives as people with the highest cost of living but rarely able to afford more than what they called their "rabbit hutch" apartments starting to be recognized? Was the box-like society beginning to squeeze its citizens out?

Chapter 12 discussed the six elements of the Japanese social contract: social solidarity, or feelings of mutual support; hierarchical social structure, determined by age seniority; role playing, for each social role one is required to play; reciprocal obligations between people in long-term relationships; putting the country (or organization, or group) before self; and approved self-censorship. What if anything happened to this social contract in 1995? There is little doubt that most Japanese feel that social solidarity was the contract element to have suffered most as a result of the events of 1995. The fact that some Japanese impersonally attacked and killed other Japanese left a deep impression. Many Japanese intellectuals soberly consider that this marked a turning point in the development of Japanese society, and fear that worse is to come. The critic and academic Shin'ichi Nakazawa (*Asahi Shinbun*, 1995) wrote that the sarin gas attacks have produced a

> massive fault-line in the spirit of the Japanese people ... that fault-line is the division that now exists between individuals and 'others' ... the plug has been pulled out that held back the violence that goes with access to the psychic realm.

According to older Japanese, social solidarity has been slowly but steadily declining over the past thirty years, but that decline was only marginal compared to what happened in 1995. Although it is too early to tell, it would not be surprising if the orderliness of Japanese society is also damaged by the scale of crimes like the sarin gas attack. Unquestioning obedience, attachment to entities larger than oneself, and the personal search for identity by young Japanese are also likely to be affected. These may be intensified, and, as some Japanese writers have forecast, move the Japanese people further to the right toward a readiness to accept more authoritarianism and a more fascist type of government.

The 1995 disasters occurred at the end of a long period of economic and social malaise and uncertainty which contrasted greatly with Japan's economic miracle and burgeoning affluence of earlier years. Psychologically, many Japanese commentators observed, the Japanese people were not ready for what was happening. They were too *heiwa boke*, or *anzen boke* (overindulged in or bemused by peace and security), implying that they were still living in an innocent, peaceful, secure past instead of facing up to the new reality.

In retrospect, maybe it seemed that the Japanese, proud of their achievements and often arrogant in their commercial dealings, had been "riding for a fall." As in *Othello*, had some Iago-like cosmic villain been waiting in the wings to bring the Japanese Othello down into the dust at the very height of its triumphs and achievements? The period 1990–95 saw the bursting of the so-called bubble economy, when stock prices, real estate values, and corporate profits plummeted, Japan's banks were left with trillions of dollars in debts that would never be paid back, the continual strengthening of the yen relentlessly countered all efforts to climb out of recession, the United States demanded ever more stridently that Japan open its markets and reduce its balance of payments surplus, and shocking crimes occurred, especially public assassinations (or attempts) of journalists, businessmen, bankers, policemen, and people accused of heinous crimes, which were out of character with the secure image of the country.

Even before the Great Hanshin Earthquake and the sarin gas attacks, there was a widespread sense of foreboding. Fears of imminent disaster have been pervasive in Japan for thirty years or more. In the 1970s a book entitled *Japan Sinks* by Sakyo Komatsu touched a nerve of deep insecurity in many Japanese who had an underlying fear that Japan was an unstable country (Sugimoto, 1983). The prophecies of Nostradamus were first translated into Japanese in the mid-1970s, and their message of more or less impending doom continue to be read by and influence many Japanese. In the 1980s, a book that predicted that Mount Fuji would explode and a great earthquake devastate Tokyo on a specific date sold several hundred thousand copies; an estimated 50,000 people relocated to outlying districts in the months preceding that date. Also in the 1980s, the Unification Church (the Moonies) was responsible for swindling many Japanese in door-to-door sales of overpriced religious artifacts said to placate dissatisfied ancestors bringing misfortune to the family. This scam was eventually stopped by a change in the law in regard to door-to-door sales, and a government inquiry into the circumstances of Unification Church activities. From the 1980s to the present, various sects of Buddhism, including some especially created for the purpose, have enriched themselves enormously at the expense of the millions of women who had had abortions but had not taken the "proper" steps, such as arranging Buddhist services for the dead and other memorial rites, to appease the souls of their unborn children.

TRADITIONAL MYTHS VERSUS MODERN RATIONALISM

The mid-1980s marked the beginning of an occult boom that continues to show no signs of peaking. Japanese started to show a greater interest in occult Buddhism and in all the trappings of the occult boom in the West such as tarot, fortune telling, astrology, crystals, palmistry, phrenology, divination, "visions," levitation, telepathy, parapsychology, spirit possession, and spirit communication, as well as beliefs associated with these. But it should not be supposed that the occult is something alien to the Japanese: ancient records indicate that beliefs in spirits, magic, mystery, and miracles were widespread.

According to Japan's origin myths, the country was created by a female god and a male god, Izanami and Izanagi, who then produced countless other *kami* (gods) to populate Japan. While giving birth to the fire god, Izanami died. Grief-stricken, Izanagi followed her to the underworld, a hell of putrid and decaying bodies, only to find that she attacked him and tried to immerse him in the horrid putrescence. Izanangi barely managed to escape by rolling a large rock onto the border between the world of life and the underworld of death. Izanami was enraged by this and threatened that if the rock were not removed she would cause one thousand people in the land of the living to die each day. Izanagi thereupon retorted that he would cause one thousand five hundred people to be born each day. This myth embodies the fundamental concepts and images for Japanese ideas of the nature of spiritual reality. Elements of these feature prominently in Haruki Murakami's novel *The Hard-boiled Wonderland and the End of the World* (1991), which is seen as an allegory of modern Japan, and in some aspects of the occult boom.

Gods have been constantly created by the Japanese. They have always included natural objects such as mountains, but many are the deceased, especially one's own ancestors. These gods can be forces for good, such as Tenjin, the god of learning and education still venerated and prayed to today for success in study (there are Tenjin temples all over Japan where millions flock prior to examinations, not to mention statues of Tenjin in many homes). In real life he was the famous ninth-century scholar Sugawara Michizane. Ian Reader (1991) reported how he came to be canonized as Tenjin:

> Sugawara fell victim to political intrigue and was sent into exile, where he died unhappily. Shortly after, a series of misfortunes struck the capital Kyoto: these were interpreted as caused by his angry and vengeful spirit seeking recompense for the wrongs inflicted upon him in life. Consequently the Court decided to appease him by building him a shrine and venerating him as a *kami*.... Because of his scholastic ability it was natural that he should become a *kami* of learning.

This story and the original creation myth clearly indicate a Japanese belief in the powers and malevolence of "spirits" that persists today barely concealed under a veneer of rationalism. The post-1945 era has seen the rise of rationalism derived from Western science and philosophy which emphasizes individualism and the use of logic and scientifically grounded principles to understand and explain natural and social phenomena. Japanese rationalism exists side by side with a caring concern for the impact of rationalistic policies on individuals, unlike in the West where concern for the impact of policies on individuals is largely the responsibility of lobby groups or those philanthropically inclined.

Business and government are the most rationalistic domains in Japan and therefore the domains where religion and superstition have the least sway. Even so, government directly or indirectly perpetuates national religious events, such as coronations, national Shinto rites, care of Ise Shrine, etc. Some but not all businesses also perpetuate religion by giving reverence to and worshipping statues of their founders or ancestors. One still finds businesses with a *kamidana* (shrine) set up within the president's office where offerings are made to ancestors and their advice sought. Surveys today, however, show that only half the Japanese believe that the spirit lives on after death; although no figures are available on beliefs in the past, this must represent a great decline from prewar days, and thus a significant victory for rationalism.

The very fact of Japan's rampant religiosity, as seen in the vigor and variety of new religions, suggests that rationality does not compete with spiritualism but coexists with it. Spiritualism flourishes in pluralistic Japan because it draws upon traditions and customs critical to the identity of the Japanese. Ritual purity, respect for ancestors and for the past, and widespread traditional belief in kindly spirits and malevolent ghosts are part of a rich social context. The myriad closed organizations and groups and a central philosophy that demands lifelong commitment by each individual to something larger than oneself hinge upon a recognition of individual powerlessness. Although many Japanese deny that they are religious, I consider that they are merely saying something about their lack of religious beliefs and practices. Japanese society and culture inherently acclimate most members to a religious orientation (albeit nonuniversal). Professor Tetsuo Yamaori (1995) comments, "When most Japanese say they are atheist, they feel a twinge in the pit of their stomachs, for they are aware that they believe in both god and Buddha ... that the Japanese attitude had [traditionally] been pantheistic."

One new cult religion, Agonshu, founded in 1978, appeals to the Japanese due to its concern with appeasing the unhappy spirits of the dead, which Agonshu, like most Japanese cults and individuals, claims can afflict the living both physically and spiritually. Appeasement of unhappy spirits occurs during Agonshu's twice yearly fire rites, when in front of a live and television audience of millions two giant bonfires of pine branches are lit. These are fed regularly with large bundles of wooden sticks on which believers have written prayers, wishes, or invocations; the bonfires are ablaze the whole day. Other major sects (such as Mahikari, or True Light) believe that all illness is due to possession and pollution by an unhappy spirit, and that the major task of the religion is to confront and exorcise that spirit.

GROUPISM AND THE YOUNG

The principal way to survive and enjoy life in Japan is to become part of a permanent group where one can feel secure and accepted. But there is a price to be paid for permanent membership in a group in the form of exclusive commitment and submission to superiors and the overriding group philosophy. It is forbidden to have close relationships with members of "competing" groups. Commitment to the group is reinforced by developing mutual obligations with other group members, forming attachments to and dependence on others, receiving a salary that permits one to live with modest comfort, and enjoying the rapport and affinity one builds up with other members.

This model has not broken down in Japan. Membership in social, commercial, and industrial groups still provides all these functions. What has changed is that a greater variety of groups has developed and groups are more polarized from the ethics and values of mainstream society. Japan is today a highly pluralized society. In 1945, most Japanese still believed in the feudal samurai philosophy of putting service to the country first. With time, service to the country declined, and service to one's company came to dominate. In 1995, service to the country still thrills the hearts of some business leaders and some students in top universities (who alone have a chance to become government officials), but otherwise receives scant attention. The ethic of serving the company is becoming weaker among young people, who have a more skeptical and rational view of employment and employers.

Part of the problem in traditional membership groups in Japan is that young entrants into the group, as part of their demonstration of personal flexibility and humility, are expected to do any task assigned. Those who choose an academic career and enter a postgraduate research program are not able to choose a research topic or area but are assigned an area by a supervisor. There is virtually no chance of changing either supervisor or discipline. This system ensures that most young members of Japan's task-oriented society do not enjoy satisfying or rewarding work as a matter of deliberate policy. Many work in big organizations that are rationalized, depersonalized breeding grounds of powerlessness or suppressed, unfocused rage. If individuals are not singled out as fast-track candidates for senior management positions, or do not become "yes-people" or fawning followers, there is little left except private alienation from mainstream society. The alternative options are unthinkable for most Japanese: working as an independent or free-lancer, living abroad, or joining a cult or other marginal group. How unthinkable dropping out remains is illustrated in the following story, told by Patrick Carney, who spent three years working in a leading Japanese bank:

> When I arrived in my new department I sat next to Uchida, an interesting twenty-eight-year-old Japanese who had just returned from Stanford [University] where, at the bank's expense, he had taken an MBA. He was very outspoken. He would phone his buddies in the US and speak in a very loud voice. But his biggest crime was to argue with Sugai, our assistant manager, the most powerful guy in our department, and a bit of a peacock who thought highly of himself. Uchida would stand in front of Sugai's desk and give his opinions in a rather loud voice.
>
> After two months, Uchida was transferred and I saw no more of him, but rumors kept circulating. For instance, the bank tried to sack him on psychological grounds, apparently because in that way they wouldn't have to pay him a pension. Again, we heard that his wife was trying to divorce him. Eventually, we heard nothing, and I assumed he had been transferred somewhere.
>
> One day I got a phone call from a foreigner asking for Uchida. I asked our secretary where he was. She said, "*Nakunarimashita.*" I thought ... it means, "he's dead." No, that's too strange, it must be a euphemism for, "He's been fired." But after pondering a while, I realized it had to mean,

"he's dead." I couldn't believe it. "Is he dead?" I asked her. "Yes," she said. I thought, "What am I going to say to this guy?" But I just said, "Sorry, I don't know how to get hold of him."

Then I asked the secretary, "Did he commit suicide?" Yes, she said. How did you know? Hey, someone twenty-eight, looking pretty healthy when I saw him last, doesn't usually drop dead. She finished our conversation by saying, "Well, that's what I've heard." Later that day, I approached the nicest man in our division. I knew if I was going to get a straight answer, it would be from him. "Is Uchida dead?" I asked. "Yes," he said. That was it.

It suddenly struck me how cold the Japanese are. Once you're out of the group, that's it. He had been erased from the corporate collective memory. They were always sending notices around saying somebody's mother or father had passed away, and giving details of the funeral arrangements. But for Uchida—nothing. He had disappeared from the face of the earth. His name was never mentioned again.

This anecdote illustrates the in-group/out-group orientation so common in Japanese organizations. "In" is warm, caring, concerned, while "out" signifies a void. Some Japanese intellectuals do not regard the warm, caring in-group orientation of Japanese organizations as attractive. Rather, they claim that such groups are independent and in conflict with others, and that a society made up of such organizations provides no basis for developing a mature society of individuals who get along well with one another.

Another aspect of the life and psychology of young people in Japan (and elsewhere) is an idealistic, melodramatic view of life as a struggle between good and evil. The brightest, most idealistic of the young want to change the world. They are dissatisfied with the adult, established world that has no place for them and where they are not recognized. On the other hand, the young in Japan have questing, curious minds, question the conventional, feel themselves to be special and exceptional, and have a strong sense of what they are able to do in the world. As the Japanese intellectual Toriaki Asabane reported in the *Asahi Shinbun* (1995) "Young Japanese discover that they are nobody, but underneath is the sense that they have a special mission in life, that their existence is special, and that their story ultimately excels that of all others." Such narcissism is a significant platform for the desire to save the world that is so common in Japan, even though "saving the world" really means "reforming Japanese society." The writer Yushi Shimada, writing in the *Mainichi Shinbun* (1995) about the young people today to whom Aum Shinrikyō and the study of the occult have such appeal, phrased it thus, "One is a warrior in the middle of the millenarian battle to save mankind fought between good and evil." But this kind of melodramatic view of life and its meaning is a serious mental barrier to emotional maturity.

Young Japanese can be easily offended and resentful when their qualities and potential are not recognized. They inherit a world where status and rank vary so subtly that it is easy for the best and brightest to feel that they are trapped in a social maze that cannot really be justified, especially when one looks at the "simpler" societies of the West. These characteristics, plus the inner need to be recognized, become a platform on which the appeal of a cult, such as Aum Shinrikyō, can be easily established. They also form a major barrier to the reintegration of cult members into society.

The disappearance of a unifying national goal, the decline of integrated family life, the rise of an affluent, independent, well-educated youth that shares few values with older generations, and the occurrence of terrorist acts and assassinations are just some of the factors that have made traditional generalizations about Japanese society seem dated and even inapplicable. Such generalizations are being qualified and questioned. The general interest of non-Japanese until this time has focused on the business sector and ways of thinking of Japanese businesspeople. They have presented the most clearly rationalized face of Japan, making it easy to underestimate the extent of nonrational behavior and thought in other domains of Japanese culture.

THE AUM SHINRIKYŌ AFFAIR

Before it was decertified, Aum was one of some 180,000 organizations in Japan registered by the government as an official religious body. As such, it was entitled to tax-free status and freedom of operation that critics are now labeling "extraterritoriality." Aum showed great entrepreneurial spirit, establishing successful businesses in computer retailing and printing. Established in 1982 by the half-blind acupuncturist and yoga teacher Chizuo Matsumoto, who later changed his name to Shoko Asahara, Aum on the surface seemed disarmingly ordinary and harmless, if at the same time technologically sophisticated for a religious organization. Aum had at most 10,000 adherents, a small number compared with Soka Gakkai, the largest of the new religions in Japan with its seven million-plus members, own political party, and own daily newspaper. The public face of Aum in Japan was their hundred or so suburban and regional offices and businesses, featuring large signs advertising the name of the cult, making it a part of everyday life for millions of Japanese. Its headquarters in the village of Kamikuisshiki at the foot of Mount Fuji was a compound of nondescript buildings which echoed the harmless appearance of its members.

Ritual training and discipline were important aspects of Aum. Purification was central, and involved fasting with daily purging using large quantities of hot water, meditation in the lotus position, and cathartic breathing meditations. In everyday life, Aum members wore casual clothes or sports training outfits. Only within their own compounds did they wear the white gowns or electronic headgear that have been photographed so often. The headgear was meant to suppress the members' own brain waves so that they could tune into the brain waves of their master, Shoko Asahara. Nor was it just his brain waves that were desired. Followers wore masks of his face when they supported him in his one attempt at being elected to political office. His hair clippings, nail parings, and bath water, not to mention semen, were treasured, and potions made from these were sold to devotees for very high prices.

Asahara, like many Japanese religious leaders, was treated by his disciples with greater reverence than royalty. He could not be touched or even approached. Central to his mandate as a religious leader was his possession of superpowers, especially his ability to levitate. He condemned Japanese society as vacuous and meaningless and offered instead a nontraditional, esoteric philosophy of life. His claim that Aum was "a source stream of Tibetan esoteric Buddhism" was especially appealing to intelligent young people interested in the esoteric. His appeal to young Japanese was totally novel: He was a blind, young, society-rejecting, levitating leader with Indian spiritual experience, an attractive appearance, and an eclectic set of beliefs that sounded universal and profound.

It is easy to see connections between Aum practices and beliefs and those of other Japanese institutions. Most central is the technocratic image. Aum offered an ascetic life that led to superpowers gained through technology. The cult had laboratories, scientists, computer businesses, electronic headgear, and searchers for truth in a high-tech age. Organization was the other prominent feature of Aum as viewed from the outside. There were thirteen spiritual levels for members, with Asahara at the highest level and his fifteen elite leaders occupying the next two ranks. The cult was organized along the lines of an alternative Japanese government, with the same ministries. The Dalai Lama, commenting on his one meeting with Asahara in 1990 (*Sydney Morning Herald*), said that, in his opinion, Asahara spent too much time on thinking about his organization and too little on practice.

Aum in reality was an organization that developed from an apparently harmless cult (in 1990, Asahara said no more than "I am the Christ") into one that by 1993 was focused on bringing about the millenarian prophecies of its leader. By 1994, Asahara had declared that his intention was to conquer Japan. The first sarin gas attack on March 23, 1995, was regarded by the cult as only a trial run. The major plan for October 1995 called for a ton of sarin gas to be dropped by cult-owned helicopters on the Diet Building and others in the government district of Kasumigaseki, with an invasion later that day of ostensible aid workers from Russia, who would in fact be armed Aum cult warriors.

A bizarre but equally interesting future was mapped out in notes found on Masami Tsuchiya, head of Aum's chemical arms unit, when he was arrested. *The Guardian Weekly* (May 21, 1995) published the following on those notes:

> Asahara will be imprisoned in the 1990s, but his trial will prove the existence of supernatural power and all 100 million Japanese will become followers of Aum.... Aum would become more powerful than the state in 1995 and it would advance into Jerusalem and be tortured by heretics in 1998–9, but the growing military might of Aum would rescue its disciples. After a final world war, Tsuchiya would help rebuild Japan into a kingdom that would last 1,000 years.

Asahara attracted top young scientists from leading universities and allowed them to work freely in the cult's laboratories. While they were all apparently from "good" homes, they were also inexperienced, ideological (that is, not pragmatic), and with no previous religious interest. Asahara's eulogizing of Hitler was well received by many young Japanese. He told his followers that Hitler was a great man, the best diplomat in the twentieth centruy, and a clever, charismatic leader. Sarin gas had an obvious fascination for Asahara, presumably because it was tested by Nazis in their death camps (and also used by Saddam Hussein to annihilate Kurdish villagers). Asahara mentioned sarin a number of times in talks and sermons during 1994 (a year before the attacks), and also accused unspecified enemies of using sarin against Aum during 1994.

One of the central precepts that Asahara communicated to his sect was, *"Kyōdan wa kokka o shinogu"* (the sect is greater than the state). The practical outcome of this premise was to underwrite the paternalism of the sect toward its members, showing its dependence upon the value of paternalism by organizations which exists in Japanese society generally. But it came to justify everything done legally and illegally by cult members, as well as to justify the total commitment to Aum that members were required to give. For example, when people became Aum Shinrikyō members, they had to make wills leaving the disposition of their entire estate to the cult, as well as listing all of their assets which had to be immediately given over. By early 1995, according to one member, the total worth of the cult was ¥100 billion (US$1.18 billion). In manufacturing sarin gas, Aum broke laws relating to the purchase of raw materials, and used dummy companies to buy them so that the Aum connection would not be revealed to outsiders.

The evidence seems clear that Aum did not tolerate escape. Many were interned, isolated, or put under "house arrest" in rooms without windows or punished by being forced to drink twelve liters of water a day through a three-centimeter tube inserted in the throat, vomiting after each drink, and continuing until the feces became transparent. Dangerous critics and turncoats were kidnapped and murdered. Twelve bodies were found under one of the Kamikuishiki buildings. It is not clear at this time what the circumstances were surrounding the death of these people. There is evidence that some Aum members were killed during the administration to them of electric shock, the aim of which was to wipe out their memories, to give them a new psychic start (the resemblance to a similar notion in Murakami's 1991 novel, reviewed at the end of this chapter, is so striking as to appear more than coincidence). Precedents already existed for the murder of "turncoats" in Japan: Red Army terrorists in the 1970s killed or lynched fourteen of their members who had threatened to leave the group. This can be seen as an extension of the widespread belief that one makes a commitment to membership in one group for life, that lifelong commitment is irreversible, and that the breaking of it is not merely disloyal but immoral.

At the Kamikuisshiki headquarters Aum had set up a factory to produce small arms. It tried to buy missiles and nuclear technology in Russia. Military training with small arms was a requirement for many Aum members. Up to forty members were involved in the production, distribution, and ultimate delivery of sarin gas to the discharge points. Members of Aum in the Self-Defense Forces were arrested for passing classified data on chemical weapons and other military matters, as well as for unauthorized weapons handling and breaking and entering. The Mitsubishi Research Institute was also burgled for technological secrets on laser weapons by cult members. Aum practice reflects the point made in Chapter 12 that Japanese ascetic life is inward, not ethical. Most Japanese believe that if one is acting unselfishly for the sake of the organization or group, then one is behaving ethically. Larger questions and decisions in relation to universal values or the outside world are left to the leader.

SPECULATION ABOUT THE FUTURE

Ordinary people in Japan had their fears confirmed by what they learned about Aum: awesome, hidden centers of vast power exist in Japan in mysterious but real places. The members of the Aum power center were remote and detached from society, alienated from the values of mainstream Japan, with a nihilistic ethic of intellectualized, depersonalized aggression against the outside world. In their apocalyptic view of the world, only they would survive. Everyone else was expendable. Thus Aum used ethical and spiritual discipline as a means not for the spiritual realization of individual members, but to promote the world-destroying vision of one man.

In this respect, the story of Aum is a salutary warning to Japan. Aum is first of all a classic example of a utopia of the kind described in Chapter 6. It was under tight control by a man who shared some of the arrogance of samurai administrators in feudal days, that is, he despised the "people" and saw anyone who failed to make a lifelong commitment to Aum as expendable. The similarities to the past are troubling, for they show that chauvinistic Japanese values still have a life of their own.

As noted at the end of Chapter 12, one of the most serious concerns about Japanese society is its lack of universal ethical standards, the development of which is suppressed by loyalty to the immediate group or organization. The story of Aum is yet another confirmation of how Japanese group life can ethically desensitize the individual with possibly life-threatening outcomes, and a warning that even worse horrors have the potential to occur in Japan, not least of all the reemergence of a fascist political party bent on chauvinistic adventurism.

AN ALLEGORY OF MODERN JAPAN: THE HARD-BOILED WONDERLAND AND THE END OF THE WORLD

How contemporary the Japanese belief in spirts remains is illustrated in the novels of one of Japan's leading writers, Haruki Murakami, and especially in his novel *The Hard-Boiled Wonderland and the End of the World.* Set in present-day Tokyo, this book presents us with a Japanese version of George Orwell's *1984*, but one in which everything now known about Aum Shinrikyō, Asahara Shoko, and his prophecies about the end of the world seems consistent with Murakami's fictional cyberpunk world of heroes and villains.

Murakami used many devices in his novel that tap the mood of the times and the myths and the cultural background in Japan. These include the following:

1. An indeterminate border exists between the world of ordinary people and the underworld of the malevolent "Inklings." This corresponds symbolically to the large rock rolled across the border between the world of life and that of death in the Izanagi myth.
2. The Inklings are projections of the fear of ordinary Japanese of invisible forces in the dark or hidden

interstices of the world; at one level, they represent dark-
ness and evil consistent with Japanese myth, while at
another level they represent a cluster of vague fears of
contamination that plague many Japanese today.

3. The impersonal presentation of characters without
   names, whose identity is thus marginalized, and of
   ambiguous organizations that sacrifice people for the
   purposes of "science" appear to be denouncements by
   Murakami of the impersonality of organizational life in
   Japan. They are also reminiscent of Aum's ambiguity, its
   marginalization of nonmembers, and its apparent readiness to sacrifice people who interfered with the achievement of its goals.

4. The "end of the world" concept both agonizes and
   bemuses the central character in the novel. Asahara has
   made many prophecies of a coming Armageddon.

5. A picture is painted of organizations in ruthless competition with one another, ready to steal technology and
   ideas for profit. This is a thinly disguised landscape of
   the Japanese corporate world, in which industrial espionage is widespread. There are obvious parallels with
   Aum's attempts to steal technological know-how.

6. The detailed account of mind-altering techniques is an
   apt if fictional parallel to what Aum attempted among its
   members, including the problems such altered individuals experience when they eventually try to return to
   "ordinary" life.

Bibliography

Aida, Yuji.

Asabane, Toriaki.

Asahi Shinbun.

Asami, Sadao.

Bayley, David H.

Becker, C. B.

Ben-Arif, Eyal, et al.

Benedict, R.

Blacker, Carmen.

Blaker, Michael K.

Nihonjin no Ishiki Kōzō (The structure of Japanese consciousness). 1970.

Asahi Shinbun. May 15, 1995.

May 15, 1995, by Toriaki Asabane.
——June 8, 1995, by Sun'ichi Nakazawa.

Genri Undō—Tōitsukai no Seitai (A movement of principle. The real face of the Unification Church). Tokyo: Banshosha, 1989.

Forces of Order. Berkeley: University of California Press, 1976.

"Reasons for the Lack of Argumentation and Debate in the Far East." *International Journal of Intercultural Relations* 10 (1986): 75–92.

Unwrapping Japan. Manchester, UK: Manchester University Press, 1990.

The Chrysanthemum and the Sword. Rutland, VT, and Tokyo: Charles E. Tuttle, 1946.

The Catalpa Bow: A Study of Shamanistic Practices in Japan. London: Allen and Unwin, 1983.

Evaluating Japanese Diplomatic Performance. Project on Japanese Foreign Policy, East Asian Institute, Columbia University, undated.
——*Japan's International Negotiating Style.* New York: Columbia University Press, 1977.

Blyth, R. H.   *Zen in English Literature and Oriental Classics.* Tokyo: Hokuseido, 1942.
——*Haiku.* Tokyo: Hakuseido, 1949.

Braddon, R.   *The Other Hundred Years War.* London: Collins, 1983.

Buruma, Ian.   *A Japanese Mirror: Heroes and Villains of Japanese Culture.* London: Penguin, 1984.

Clark, Gregory.   "No Formula for Success." *Speaking of Japan* (July 1986): 22–26.

Collcutt, M., et al.   *Cultural Atlas of Japan.* Oxford: Phaidon-Oxford, 1990.

Daikichi, I.   "The Survival Struggle of the Japanese Community." *Japan Interpreter*, 9:4 (Spring 1975): 466–494.

Deacon, R.   *Kempei Tai: A History of the Japanese Secret Service.* New York: Berkeley Books, 1983.

De Vos, G.   *Socialization for Achievement.* Berkeley: University of California Press, 1973.

Dore, R.   *Taking Japan Seriously.* Palo Alto, CA: Stanford University Press, 1987.

Dower, J. W.   *Origin of the Modern Japanese State: Selected Writings of E. H. Norman.* New York: Pantheon Books, 1975.

Fairbank, J. K., et al.   *East Asia: Tradition and Transformation.* New York: Houghton Mifflin, 1973.

Fallows, J.   "Containing Japan." *The Atlantic Monthly* (May 1989): 40–54.

Field, Norma.   *In the Realm of a Dying Emperor.* New York: Pantheon, 1991.

Fields, George.   *From Bonsai to Levi's.* New York: MacMillan, 1983.

Finkelstein, B., et al (eds.).   *Transcending Stereotypes: Discovering Japanese Culture and Education.* Yarmouth, ME: Intercultural Press, 1991.

Gendai.   "Itoh Motoko Zen Kokuhaku" (The Complete Confession of Motoko Itoh). July 1986, pp. 96–112. Monthly magazine. Tokyo: Kodansha.

Greenfield, K.	*The Nation.* Cited in *Japan Free Press,* October 28, 1991.
Hamabata, M. M.	*Crested Kimono.* Ithaca, NY: Cornell University Press, 1990.
Hane, Mikiso.	*Peasants, Rebels & Outcastes: The Underside of Modern Japan.* New York: Pantheon, 1982.
Hasegawa, K.	*Japanese Style Management.* Tokyo: Kodansha International, 1986.
Hayashi, S.	*Culture and Management in Japan.* Tokyo: University of Tokyo Press, 1988. ——"Hearings Shed Light on Money for Favors." *Japan Access* III: 8 (March 2, 1992).
Hirschmeier, J., and T. Yui.	*The Development of Japanese Business.* Cambridge, MA: Harvard University Press, 1975.
Hoyt, Edwin.	*The Kamikazes.* New York: Robert Hale, 1984.
Hunter, James.	"Truth and Effectiveness in Revelatory Stories." *Revision* 6:2 (Fall 1983): 3–15.
Idemitsu, S.	*Eien no Nihon* (Eternal Japan). Tokyo: Heibonsha, 1975.
Imai, Masaaki.	*Kaizen.* Tokyo: Japan Productivity Center, 1989.
Japan Economic Institute.	*Japanese Corporate Management: Does It Need To Be Changed?* April 17, 1992.
Japan Free Press.	1991; 39: 154.
Johnston, C.	"*Omote* (explicit) and *Ura* (implicit): Translating Japanese Political Terms." *Journal of Japanese Studies* 6:1 (Winter 1980): 85–115.
Kanter, R. M.	*Commitment and Community: Communes and Utopias in Sociological Perspective.* Cambridge, MA: Harvard University Press, 1972.
Kitagawa, J. M.	*On Understanding Japanese Religion.* Princeton. NJ: Princeton University Press, 1987.

Kunihiro, M.   *Nihonjin wa Kokusaijin ni Nareruka?* (Can the Japanese become international people?). Tokyo: Seikyo Shinbunsha, 1980.

Kyogoku, Jun'ichi.   "Modernization and National Ethos." *Japan Foundation Newsletter*, Vol. XIII, No. 3, October 1985.

Lebra, T. S.   *Above the Clouds: Status Culture of the Modern Japanese Nobility.* Berkeley: University of California Press, 1991.

Lee, O-Young.   *Smaller Is Better.* Tokyo and New York: Kodansha International, 1982.

Lu, David J.   *Inside Corporate Japan.* Tokyo: Tuttle, 1986.

McCormack, G., and Y. Sugimoto (eds.).   *Democracy in Contemporary Japan.* Sydney: Hale & Iremonger, 1986.

McCreary, Don R.   *Japanese-U.S. Business Negotiations.* New York: Praeger, 1986.

McGill, Peter.   "Career Cannibal." *Sydney Morning Herald.* June 20, 1992.

McFarland, H. N.   *The Rush Hour of the Gods.* New York: Harper Colophon, 1967.

McKinstry, J. A., and A. N. McKinstry.   *Jinsei Annai.* New York: M. E. Sharpe Inc., 1991

Mainichi Shinbun.   June 14, 1995.

Mannari, H., and H. Befu (eds.).   *The Challenges of Japan's Internationalization.* Tokyo: Kodansha International, 1983.

March, R. M.   *Nippon no Gokai* (Japan's misunderstandings). Tokyo: Keizaikai, 1986.
——*The Japanese Negotiator.* Tokyo: Kodansha International, 1988.
——*Honoring the Customer: Marketing and Selling to the Japanese.* Appleton, WI: John Wiley & Son, 1990.
——*Working For A Japanese Company.* Tokyo: Kodansha International, 1992.

Maruyama, Magoroh.   "Keiei no Bunka Jinruigaku" (The cultural anthropology of management). *Riso* 597 (February 1983): 144–158.

Maruyama, Masao.   "The New Logic of Japan's Young Generation."

Technological Forecasting and Social Change 28 (1985): 351–364.

Matsumoto, K.   *The Rise of the Japanese Corporate System.* London: Kegan Paul, 1991.

Matsumoto, M.   *Haragei.* Tokyo: Bunseido, 1978.

Mishima, Y.   *On Hagakure.* London: Penguin, 1979.

Miyanaga, Kuniko.   *Social Reproduction and Transcendence.* Doctoral Dissertation. Vancouver: University of British Columbia, 1983.

Mizuno, J.   *The Japanese Liking for Circles.* Tokyo: Kenkyusha, 1984.

Moloney, J. M.   *Understanding the Japanese Mind.* Tokyo: Tuttle, 1975.

Morioka, K.   *Gekiron Kigyosha kai: Karōshi to Hataraki-kata o Kangaeru.* Tokyo: Iwanami, 1995.

Mouer, R., and Y. Sugimoto.   *Images of Japanese Society.* London: Kegan Paul, 1986.

Murakami, H.   *The Hard-Boiled Wonderland and the End of the World.* Tokyo: Kodansha International, 1991.

Nakamura, Hajime.   "Basic Features of the Legal, Political, & Economic Thought of Japan." In *The Japanese Mind*, ed. C. A. Moore. Honolulu: University of Hawaii Press, 1967.

Nakane, C.   *Japanese Society.* London: Penguin, 1970.

Nakazawa, Shin'ichi.   *Asahi Shinbun.* June 8, 1995.

Namba, P.   "Sensory Cues to Cultural Identity." Research paper, Aoyama Gakuin University, Tokyo, December 16, 1987 (photocopy).

Neumann, W. L.   *America Encounters Japan.* Baltimore, MD: Johns Hopkins Press, 1963.

NTT Mediascope.   *Everything You Ever Wanted to Know about Business Tsukiai.* Tokyo: HCI Publications, 1991.

Ohnuki-Tierney, E.   *Illness & Culture in Contemporary Japan: An Anthropological View.* London: Cambridge: Cambridge University Press, 1984.

	—The Monkey as Mirror. Princeton, NJ: Princeton University Press, 1987.
Okonogi, K.	"The Ajase Complex of the Japanese." Japan Echo (1978): 88–105.
Okumura, Hiroshi.	"The Closed Nature of Japanese Intercorporate Relations." Japan Echo (1982): 53–61.
Ouchi, William.	Theory Z: How American Business Can Meet the Japanese Challenge. New York: Avon, 1981.
Passin, H.	Japanese and the Japanese. Tokyo: Kinseido, 1980.
Pharr, S. J.	Losing Face: Status Politics in Japan. Berkeley: University of California Press, 1990.
Plath, David (ed.).	Work and Lifespace in Japan. Stoneybrook, NY: State University of New York Press, 1983.
Reader, I.	Religion in Contemporary Japan. London: Macmillan, 1991.
Rohlen, T. P.	For Harmony and Strength. Berkeley: University of California Press, 1974.
	—"Order in Japanese Society: Attachment, Authority and Routine." Journal of Japanese Studies 15:1 (Winter 1989): 5–40.
Seward, J., and H. Van Zandt.	Japan: The Hungry Guest. Tokyo: Yohan, 1985.
Sheldon, C. D.	The Rise of the Merchant Class in Tokugawa Japan. London: Russell & Russell, 1973.
Shimada, H.	"The Desperate Need for New Values in Japanese Corporate Behavior." Journal of Japanese Studies 17:1 (1991): 107–125.
Shimada, Yushi.	Mainichi Shinbun. May 15, 1995.
Singer, Kurt.	Mirror, Sword, and Jewel. London: Croom Helm, 1973.
Smith, R. J., and Ella Wiswell.	The Women of Suye Mura. Chicago: University of Chicago Press, 1982.
Sono, F.	Stages of Growth: Reflections on Life and Management. Tokyo: TDK Electronics, 1981.

Sugimoto, Y.

Chō-kanri retto Nippon (The ultra-controlled Japanese archipelago). Tokyo: Kobunsha, 1983.

Sullivan, J. J.

"A Critique of Theory Z." *Academy of Management Review* 8:1 (1983): 132–142.

Suzuki, D. T.

Zen and Japanese Culture. Princeton, NJ: Princeton University Press, 1959.

Sydney Morning Herald.

"What Japan Remembers." June 20, 1992.
——"Dalai Lama on Cult Leader." June 10, 1995.

Taylor, Jared.

Shadows of the Rising Sun. Tokyo: Tuttle, 1983.

Trucco, H.

"Uniforms." *Intersect* (January 1991): 3–8.

Upham, F. K.

"The Man Who Would Import..." [re Taiji Satoh]. *Journal of Japanese Studies* 17:2 (1991): 323–343.

Veblen, Thorsten.

Theory of the Leisure Class. London: Unwin, 1925.

Vogel, Ezra F.

Japan as No. 1. Tokyo: Tuttle, 1979.

Wakabayashi, B. T.

Anti-foreignism and Western Learning in Early Modern Japan. Cambridge, MA: Harvard University Press, 1991.

Watanabe, S.

In *Giri to Ninjō*, ed. Y. Akatsuka. Tokyo: Shodensha, 1971.

van Wolferen, Karel.

The Enigma of Japanese Power. London: McMillan, 1989.

Yamamoto, S., et al.

Nihonjin no Shakai Byōri (The social disease of the Japanese). Tokyo: Kodansha, 1982.

Yamamoto, Tsunetomo.

Hagakure: The Book of the Samurai. New York: Discus, 1979.

Yamaori, Tetsuo.

"Atheists by Default," *Look Japan*, August 1995, pp. 9–11.

Yoshida, Teigo.

"The Stranger as God: The Place of the Outsider in Japanese Folk Religion." *Ethnology*, 1981, Vol. 20: 87–89.

INDEX

abata ("flaws"), 143, 146
abortion, 56
addictions, in Japan, 143–44
affinity. *See* personal affinity.
Agonshu (religious sect), 185
Aida, Yuji, 76–77
AIDS, 139
Alcock, Sir Rutherford, 157
alcohol, as social lubricant, 67
analogies, in Japanese thought, 44
ancestors, shame before, 116–17
apologizing, 30
appearance and reality in Japanese
    society, 22, 28, 30, 31
Asabane, Toriaki, 189
Asami, Sadao, 56
asceticism. *See* Buddhism.
athleticism, 81–82
Aum Shinrikyō, 18, 189, 190–96;
    and sarin gas attacks, 180–81,
    191–92
authority, respect for, 37
Azuma, Toshio, 48–49

bathing, 153, 155
bento (lunchbox), 12
Blaker, Michael, 50–51, 52–53
Blyth, R.H., 152–53
body language, 128–29
body movement, 16, 70, 74, 76–81
Bon festivals, 72, 81

"bottle-keep" practice, 138
bowing, 80
box (*hako*) analogy for Japanese cul-
    ture, 12, 13, 139
boys, emotional conditioning of,
    64–65
Braddon, Russell, 42
breeding, as social interest, 61
bribery, 62, 11, 115, 120, 122
British seats on Tokyo Stock
    Exchange, 51–52
Buddhism, 15, 42, 86, 182;
    and asceticism, 144, 173–74, 177,
    178
burikko ("mannered" child), 46
business discussion, 30; *see also*
    negotiation.
business ethics, 118–22; *see also*
    ethics.
business rebate system, 113
business relationships, 22, 25–26,
    28–29, 31, 50

casual role-playing. *See* role-playing.
categorical comments, 34
censorship, 167
China, 23, 34, 82, 150, 155, 162
chopsticks, Westerners' use of, 76
Christianity, Japanese perceptions
    of, 42, 43
Clark, Gregory, 54

coercion, 146, 168
command culture, 88, 91–92
communication, 32–40;
    between Japanese and foreigners,
    32, 35–37, 38–40, 45–46, 46–47,
    130–31
companies, 87, 96–102, 103–104,
    119–20, 121–22; individual
    attachment to, 148–49
compromise, 51, 53–54
conceptual arguments, 44
Confucianism, 14, 15, 34, 42, 73, 82,
    91, 99, 104, 121, 156
conscience, appeals to, 117, 120
consensus decision-making, 175
conspicuous consumption, 107–108
context in Japanese communication,
    50
coping, as Japanese survival strat-
    egy, 50–54, 63
corruption, in Japan, 15, 17, 111,
    118–19, 122
Crichton, Michael, 17
Crocodile Dundee, 29
Crown Prince, 134

dandy, 29
dance, 81–82
dependency among Japanese, 55
diaries, kept by Japanese, 25
diplomacy, Japanese, 52–54
directness, Western, 35–37
discretion, 25
Dowager Empress, the, 26

economy, Japanese: economic bub-
    ble, 73, 113, 181–82; economic
    miracle, 87, 156
education, 48–50, 72, 73
Ee ja nai ka?, 77
emotional blackmail, 117, 168
emotional suppression, 129
Emperor, loyalty to, 89

Emperor Nintoku, 27
English language, 150–52
ethics, situational versus personal,
    62, 120; lack of in Japan, 14,
    174–75, 178, 194–95
etiquette: business, 135–36; social,
    64–65, 112
euphemisms, 32, 33; *see also* non-
    verbal communication.
Expulsion Edict (1825), 155
extreme right-wing, 26, 27

"face," 9, 11, 14, 28–31, 89,
    108–109
"face friend, 28
Fallow, James, 51
favors, giving and receiving, 15, 17,
    30, 111, 112, 115, 119, 122, 126
feigning emotions, 24, 30
female roles, 10, 65; *see also* moth-
    erhood, wives.
feudalism, 121–22, 156
flattery, 22
foreigners, and *tatemae*, 21; Japan-
    ese view of, 155, 157, 161; *see
    also gaijin* complex.
formal situations, and "face," 29
France, 49–50, 56–57
furusato (hometown) values, 141,
    154–55, 161

gaijin complex, 160–61
games, 75
genba (workplace), 149
generalists, in Japan, 14
gestures, Japanese, 33
gift-giving, 15, 17, 111–16, 122,
    126
girls, emotional conditioning of, 65
good and evil in Japanese psyche,
    188–89
gojo gojō (mutual cooperation and
    compromise), 54

Great Hanshin Earthquake, 179, 180
Greenfield, Karl, 17
grief, suppression of, 65–67
group orientation, 10–11, 55, 61, 88, 90, 91–92, 99–100, 125, 165, 167, 170, 172–73, 186–87, 188
gullibility, 17, 54–56, 62–63, 168; *see also* suggestibility.

haiku, 150, 152–53, 155
Hakuhodo, 59, 61
Hana yori dango ("Dumplings before flowers"), 29, 30–31
hanami (flower viewing), 72
hand movements, 74–76; *see also* manual skills.
harmony, 13, 112
Harvard University, 105–106, 109
Hearn, Lafcadio, 125
Hokusai, 82
homogeneity of Japanese, 13, 169
honor, 13
Hosei University, 109
hostess role, 47–48; *see also* wives, female roles.
Hunter, James, 164, 173

IBM Japan, 109
Idemitsu, Sazo, 96–97, 146, 173–74, 177
ideologies, 164, 167
Imai, Masaaki, 54
imperial family, 26, 27
Imperial Household Agency, 26, 27
income differentials, Japanese and Western, 16–17
incubation, as social interest, 61
independent thought, 55
indirect communication, 20, 35–36, 90–91; *see also* nonverbal communication.
individualism, Western, 9, 55, 165, 170

individuality, Japanese, 38, 40, 61, 170
industrial espionage, 27, 120–21
ingo (secret language), 142
inscrutability, Japanese, 69
intuition, 20, 33, 34
involved role-playing. *See* role-playing.
isshi sōden (trade secrets), 25

Japan Affinity Test, 131–33
Japan, attachment to, 147–48, 149–53
Japanese blood, and overseas Japanese, 44–45
Japanese genius, 12, 63
Japanese goodness evaluated, 163–64, 165–78
Japanese ideal, 9
Japanese language, attitudes to, 36–37, 150–53; *see also* Yamato kotoba.
Japanese national psychology, 11, 17, 170
Japanese pokerface, 67, 71
Japanese thought, 10, 11, 41
judo, 77–78
just-in-time inventory control, 138

kaizen (continuous improvement), 54, 95, 142
kamae (moment of stillness), 83
kamidana (shrine), 184
Kanemaru, Shin, 15
Kara, Juro, 57
karaoke, 72–73
karōshi (death from overwork), 144, 145–46, 173, 178
katakori (shoulder soreness), 80–81
keiretsu (conglomerate), 119
kimono, 85
kiza ("loud"), 70
Kobayashi, Yoshihiko, 49–50

Kokutai no Hongi (Fundamentals of national polity), 89
Komatsu, Sakyo, 182
kongō-za (diamond sitting), 84
Korea, 23, 27, 82, 85, 162
koshi (buttocks), 78
Kunihiro, Masao, 42
Kyogoku, Junichi, 14, 15

Law of the Sea conferences, 52–53
ledger, mental record of favors, 117–18
Lee, O-Young, 11, 83, 140
logic, in Japanese thought, 44; in organization of ideas, 49–50
love and understanding in Japan, 175–77

Macbeth, 79
McDonalds Japan, 107–108
male roles, 10, 174
manual skills, 75–76, 80
marebito god, 159, 160
maru society, 11
Maruyama, Masao, 59, 61
mass media, 71, 72
mass production, 71
massage, 80–81
Matsumoto, Michiro, 11
Mehta, Zubin, 83
messhi hōkō (destroying the self and serving others), 55
Mineshige, Miyuki, 145
Mishima, Yukio, 141–42, 146
Mitsubishi Defense Industries, 120–21
Miyazawa, Kiichi, 53, 116
Mizuno, Jun'ichi, 11
money in Japanese society, 107, 108
Morioka, Koji, 145
Morrison, 157
mortification, 93
motherhood, 65, 151–52, 153, 155

Murakami, Haruki, 183, 195–96
musculature, Japanese, 80–81
mythology, Japanese, 183, 184

Nakane, Chie, 11, 88
Namba, Patti, 128–29
naniwabushi (emotional persuasion), 44, 118
national service, 96
nationalism, 177
nattō society, 11
negotiation, 117, 118
"No," in Japanese discourse, 34–35
Noh drama, 66
Nomura, Kazuo, 26
nonverbal communication, 20, 32, 33, 34–36, 125
Norinaga, Motoori, 155
nostalgia, 153–55

obedience, 87, 89, 91, 92
obligation, 36, 111, 116–18, 119, 147, 166–67
occult, 183
Ohara, Yasuo, 157–58
o-iwai (congratulatory money), 113
Oka, Toshijiro, 83
Okita, Saburo, 52
Okonogi, Keigo, 43, 52
Olympic Games, 71, 73
organizations, culture of, 92, 93, 94–95, 122
ostracism, 118, 146
Ouchi, William, 99
Owada, Masako (Crown Princess), 105–106, 134, 143
Oxford University, 105–106

parent-child relationships, 148
party behavior in Japan, 67–68
Peace Constitution, 10
perfectionism in Japan, 16, 134, 137, 138–43, 145–46

Perry, Commodore, 158
personal affinity, with Japanese, 125–26, 127, 128–33
personal growth, 171–72
personal relationships in Japan, 31
pokerface. *See* Japanese pokerface.
politeness, 13, 24, 30, 31, 38
posture, Japanese and Western, 77–78
praise, giving, 34
precision, 70, 80, 135, 139–40
Princess Michiko, 26
professionalism, 14

questions, 34, 63

rationalism, 10, 184–85, 189–90
raw flesh, Japanese fascination with, 58
Red Army, 193
religiosity, 183–85
respect: for authority, 37; for seniors, 38
right-wing. *See* extreme right-wing.
ritual role-playing. *See* role-playing.
role flexibility, 92
role-playing, 45–48, 62, 166
rules in Japanese society, 134, 135–37, 138

sābisu ("service"), 113–14
Sagawa, Issei, 56–58
salarymen, 65, 101
samurai, 29, 64, 72, 73, 109, 140; warrior class, 156–57
school system, 74–75, 89–90
secretiveness, 24–26, 156
seiza (sitting position), 84, 85, 86
selflessness, Japanese, 16, 17, 120, 167
self-expression, 64–65, 69, 72, 73
self-sacrifice, 11, 88, 95, 120
self-suppression, 37, 64–65, 66, 67, 69–70, 71, 80, 87, 92–93, 146

sempai-kōhai (senior-junior) relationship, 34, 38, 134, 148, 149, 166
sennō (brainwashing), 55, 56
sentimentality, 42–44, 62, 147, 153
Seven Samurai, 159
shamans, 72
Shibata, Dr. Sui, 38–39
Shimada, Yushi, 189
Shinto, 158, 162
shyness, 67
silence, in Japanese communication, 32, 34, 37
sitting, 79, 83–86
slogans, 22–24
social coherence, 169
"social contract" for contemporary Japan, 166–67, 168
Sono, Fukujiro, 97–98
Soviet Union, 120
specialization, 14
speech-minimizing behaviors, 33
spiritualism, 185
standardized language, 37–38
status in Japan, 11, 16, 17, 37, 48, 91, 104–110, 129
strangers, 158–60
strategies: handling, 60; manic, 59; minimalist coping, 53–54; restatement, 60; risk-minimizing, 51–52; safe-niche, 61; scanning, 60; summit, 59; *see also* coping, *naniwabushi.*
suggestibility, 17, 54–56, 63, 93, 168; *see also* gullibility.
sumo, 77–78; Takanohana and Wakanohana, 141
Sun Tzu, 27
superiority, Japanese sense of, 9, 155–56, 162, 168–69
Suzuki, Daisetsu, 37
Suzuki, Takao, 42
Suzuki, Tadashi, 78–79
Suzuki, Zenko, 115–16

taboos, 26–27, 31, 56, 63
taiko mochi (professional jester), 68
tanden (stomach area), 85–86
tatami (woven mat) floors, 79, 84;
    see also sitting.
tate hiza (sitting position), 84, 85
tatemae (external appearance),
    21–25, 26, 28–31, 45, 62, 66, 88,
    145
Taylor, Jared, 42
TDK, 97–98
tears, 66
threat, bodily response to, 76–77; *see
    also* body movement.
totalitarianism in Japanese society,
    138, 166, 171
Tsukamoto, Koichi, 98
tsume (stuffing) as social symbol,
    140

Unification Church, 56, 182
uniforms, 90, 93, 137–38
United States, nation and people,
    12–13, 21, 167; relations with
    Japan, 17–18, 39
"unnatural thinking," 56–59, 63
utopian ideals in Japanese organiza-
    tions, 93–96, 99, 100–101; simi-
    larities with U.S. communes, 93

Van Wolferen, Karel, 24
Veblen, Thorsten, 107
verbal communication, 32, 33–35,
    40, 125
visitors, 135–36

Wacoal, 98
waka, 150
Watanabe, Shoichi, 151–52
Western society, 9, 12–13, 160, 167
Westerners, relations with Japanese,
    9, 14–23, 35–36, 76–77, 123–26,
    127, 155–56, 160

whaling, 43
Wiswell, Ella, 71–72, 73
wives, roles in Japan, 47–48
work ethic, 87–88, 145
working hours, 145
World War II, 10, 23, 65, 155, 156,
    157–58, 159

yakuza, 26, 27, 70
Yamato kotoba ("pure" Japanese lan-
    guage), 150–53, 155
Yasukuni Shrine, 157
yoga, 85
young generation in Japan, 59–61,
    186–87, 189

zazen (sitting Zen), 85–86
Zen Buddhism, 22, 36–37, 85, 86;
    see also Buddhism.